TALES OF A LONDON POACHER

CLEVE EDMONSTON

COVER DESIGN AND ILLUSTRATIONS
CHEYNNE EDMONSTON

Tales of a London Poacher
Updated Edition 2022
With additional material

Original Copyright 2010 Cleve Edmonston

Cover illustration Copyright Cheynne Edmonston

First Published by Coch-y-Bonduu Books LTD.
Machynlleth, Powys SY20 8DG

ISBN number 978 1 90478 429 6

All rights reserved.
No part of this publication may be reproduced, stored in a retrieval system, or transmitted in any form or by any means, electronic, mechanical, photocopying, recording or otherwise, without the prior consent of the copyright holder.

CONTENTS

Prologue	1
1. And in the Beginning	3
2. Boys, their toys and a new friend	11
3. Fishy tales	18
4. Man traps, the 'brudders' and a close call	31
5. Cut to the chase	39
6. Crazy kids and guns	46
7. New beginnings for all	52
8. Bad men and good shooting	65
9. Proper poaching	72
10. Free fresh meat	75
11. Not all coppers are bastards	81
12. Bullet points and new ground	88
13. Pest control and strange nights	96
14. Bigger game	103
15. Food for thought	110
16. Not so much a treasure map and a night on a boat	114
17. A narrow escape and grave secrets	119
18. Norfolk guns and Game Pie	125
19. Keystone cops and shooting stars	131
20. Dark waters	138
21. The spooky mansion	142
PREPARATION AND COOKING	147
Rabbit	148
Portioning	150
Rabbit Stew *(Basic)*	152
Method	153
Venison	155

Pigeon	158
Game Pie	160
With the end in sight	162
The Salt Beef Sandwich	163
A cherished memory	
Dedication and Thanks	167
Finally...	169
Roy	171

PROLOGUE

*Poaching: Encarta Dictionary; English UK (1) Catch game illegally. **To catch wild animals or fish illegally on public land or while trespassing on private land.***

With my heart racing a little faster than normal and the adrenaline beginning to flow I slowly, very slowly slid my gun into position, eased off the safety, took aim and fired! Crack went the gun and daylight became the scene as lights came on piercing the night from three different positions! Police!

1
AND IN THE BEGINNING

I entered this world on a cold January morning at a terraced house in Walthamstow in London's East End on January 16th, 1951, at number 12, The Crescent; a half-moon turning off Station Road. It was my Nan and Granddad's house and very nice too.

It had three bedrooms, a through-lounge separated by heavy red velvet curtains and a step down into the kitchen or scullery.

It also had a well-kept and good size garden that ended in a tall blank brick wall that separated the back garden from Markhouse Road School; a school that I would later attend as both an infant and then a senior, when I was 5 and then 11 years old.

My Nan kept the house lovely, as my Granddad did the garden and there was an ornamental bridge built of brick near the end that went nowhere but I remember playing on it when I was very small.

I have other childhood memories of that place, like the dark wooden walnut wardrobe with the squeaky door that frightened me as a very young child.

The smell of polish; both boot polish and lavender furniture polish I remember well, along with the clean white net curtains at the front windows and on a hot summer's day, the front door being left open, as could be done safely in those days, and the multi-coloured candy stripe streamer curtain that hung there.

The whole house had a warm, cosy feel to it, a feeling of security and cleanliness without being sterile; it was a very comforting feel.

Although too young to remember much in detail. I must have frequently been back to the Crescent during my very early years, whilst my dad, having acquired a small three-bedroom house, just five minutes' walk and three streets away, in Camden Road Walthamstow, spent all his time off, evenings and weekends, making an uninhabitable shell into a place suitable enough for both my mum and me to move into.

I had often heard the horror stories when I was older, of that house in Camden Road, and the condition it was in when my dad first took it over and got it through what was known then as *key money*.

Apparently, an old man had lived there alone for years, and the place was virtually derelict. It was an end-of-terrace house, next to a plot of waste ground and the outer wall was bowed outwardly so much that there was a four-inch gap that one could look down from the middle bedroom into the living room below.

My dad fixed this by building a false wall using plasterboard downstairs to square the room off and in so doing, created a four-inch shelf in the alcove that my Mum could keep her little brass knick-knacks on.

There was a hole apparently. in the kitchen floor that

had been made by years of wear and tear, on what would have once been solid concrete but had since turned to loose gravel and the kitchen window had angled so much, it looked as though it was something that should have belonged in the crooked house at a fairground.

This was due to the subsidence of the whole property, and to top it all, a friend of my dad came around one day, not long after he had taken over the place and said, "Eddie, you have the Red Devil here mate."

What he meant was that the place was infested with red mites. So, my old man took off all the interior doors, the waist-high half panelling in the passage, picture rails, Dado rails and any other piece of wood that was not essential and burned the lot in the garden.

He then had to have the house fumigated before we could move in. He was a real grafter my old dad and I missed him more than words can tell when on Boxing Day 1986, he died in my arms at the age of just 66.

He was what some men might call, a man's man, and although he could be a hard bastard, I was also told of him cradling me in his arms all night on more than one occasion, when, as a baby, I was a sickly child, forever suffering from chest complaints including more than once, pneumonia.

He was a character too, and I could easily write many a tale about him and the things he got up to. We, as kids, cornered a rat once in the communal garden that was now next to ours at Camden Road when the waste ground was developed, and six flats were built upon it.

"Dad! We have a rat here! Come and see!"

Now my dad never did walk much faster than a stroll at any time in his life and he came slowly out of his shed carrying a long thick threaded bolt, from what I don't know; he then leaned over the short wall separating the gardens and without a word, threw the bolt as one might throw a knife and pinned the creature to the ground, stone dead. That was my dad.

With no such thing back then, as double glazing or central heating, and the house being an end of terrace and now without many of its original interior doors, it's a wonder any of us survived winters there.

There were two open fireplaces downstairs but only ever was used, the one in the middle room. Heating the upper bedrooms was done using a single paraffin heater, placed in our bedroom, whose pattern of light coming through its vented top, cast strange patterns to dance on the ceiling.

On a winter's morning, we would sometimes wake to find ice on the *inside* of the windowpanes and with our noses frozen from being outside the sheets and blankets. On severe cold nights, over-coats were also strewn on top of our little beds.

The old dear that lived next door, Ada Bowak; was a spiritualist medium, that had a live-in lodger, Mr Thompson. Who, poor soul, had been gassed during the First World War and suffered many years of terrible coughing fits. He also had large open sores on his arms. I seem to remember.

Mrs Bowak, using her telepathic skills, apparently used to wake up a bus driver that lived miles away so he could get up for his early shift and we could sometimes hear her calling him, speaking in her own voice, then answering, in a far deeper and slower one through the thin wall that separated the houses.

On Friday nights she had meetings where expensive cars such as Daimler's and Bentley's would pull up outside and strange-looking people, some with deformities and one, I remember, with a club foot.

These people were dressed in full evening attire, would enter her house, then the heavy dark blue velvet curtains of her front room window were drawn, and the séance would start. It was truly creepy stuff!

When poor old Mr Thompson died, Mrs Bowak went on for a few more years living there alone, and my mum used to know whether she was still okay by the sound of her cleaning out her fire grate in the morning through the paper-thin walls.

However, when she had not heard anything for two days, mum sent my dad in to investigate, and he found that she had collapsed in the cold fire grate and seemed to be close to death so, called for an ambulance.

Apparently, at the hospital, nurses spent hours in just trying to clean the poor old soul up, she was so filthy, alas soon after she died.

A short time after her death, a man turned up claiming to be Mr Thompson`s son and was afraid to go into the house alone. So asked my dad to accompany him.

I tagged along and it was a weird and dirty place inside, as mice had tunnelled into a rock-hard loaf of bread that had been left on the table in the living room and although Bowak, often captured kids, my young sister for one, to make trips to the little corner shop just across the road, Bennett's. She only ever requested two items; boxes of Maltesers and packets of Gingernut biscuits of which there were many unopened packets in the house when she finally passed on.

As kids, my friend Steve lived in the house on the other side of old Mrs Bowaks` and Steve`s elder brother, Dave built him a den at the bottom of the garden made from machine part packing cases.

It was a fantastic den for us boys to hide away in and just as exciting was the tunnel we had created between our two gardens through old Bowaks` place as her garden was completely overgrown with some strange tall plants that had almost hollow stems. It was through these that we used to creep back and forth to each other's garden unseen by Bowak or Mr Thomson.

One day while in Steve`s den, smoking, as many kids did then, we thought that we were safe and away from the prying eyes of our parents when what we had not taken into account was that the exhaled smoke from our cigarettes was billowing out through the gaps of this put together structure and both my mum and Steve`s mum, Emmy, were just standing there, arms folded, laughing at the sight of this, our hapless craftiness.

We had a great childhood though, my brother and I and with Steve living next door but one, and all being much the same age, we played in the streets during the summer months and school holidays until sometimes ten `o'clock at night. When our mothers would come out and call for us to go in and we, would always ask for another five minutes of playtime.

The worse punishment I remember during those happy years was to be sent to bed early on a summer evening but to be able to hear our friends still playing outside.

My dad was always building or making things for us kids, as well as tending to the house and once he built us a jigger; a cart, made from a length of planking with a big pram frame and pram wheels on the rear and a set of large steel ball-races for front wheels.

That was some machine, and the neighbours could hear it coming down the street sounding like a train as the front metal wheels clattered and clacked over the joints in the pavement. Fully loaded I think we had about five or more kids riding this monstrous machine.

The street games we played were great too with Knock Down Ginger, cricket, football and Run Outs, being a favourite, where we used front gardens and even the underneath of parked lorries to hide from the others searching for us.

I know, it sounds frightening nowadays, but none of us got hurt; not playing that game at least, although another lad, Chris became impaled one evening on railings, and had to be lifted off by a couple of men when trying to get out of St. James` Park after he found himself locked in.

Then another couple of street kids were injured when close to one firework night they decided to put a lighted firework in a petrol tank of an old disused car and then failed to retreat to a safe distance.

There were also parks to play in. Queens Road and St James`, being the most local ones. Over the back of St, James` there was a river where we caught sticklebacks and dared one another to walk the *pipe,* a large sewer pipe that ran maybe ten feet high over a shallow river and parallel to the railway line that went from Chingford to Liverpool Street.

In those days we would be out for hours. All day sometimes, not worrying about coming home for lunch.

We would play in the derelict houses of South Grove and on surrounding waste ground or in the deserted church of St James` and the empty wooden church school of St Saviour's. This was our patch, our little manor and we loved it!

2
BOYS, THEIR TOYS AND A NEW FRIEND

For my eighth birthday, my dad bought me my very first air rifle. A Diana Model 1. I had always been mad about toy guns, what with cowboys and Indians being my favourite game to play in the street back then and while all the other kids had these silly little silver cap guns that came in cardboard holsters and fired roller caps. I had something that was as big and as heavy as the real deal. A hulking great full size, full weight Colt Peacemaker looking six-shooter that I had to open the side gate of, slide out the six bullets using the ramrod then, take each bullet apart, loading them with a couple of singular loose caps before re-assembling them, all before being able to fire off just six shots. It was great though!

My dad even made me (by hand) a holster to fit from an old leather handbag, which I still have to this day, having long since lost the original toy six-shooter.

Very many years later, I managed to find one of these *big irons*, minus the shells, at a toy fair, but would still love to get a working model of the same if I could; alas there is no makers name on it and I have failed miserably when scanning the Internet for one. Although I do believe, they were made by the Japanese Manufacturing Company (JMC) back in the 1950s?

Anyway, getting back to my first air rifle. It was just about as awkward, and time-consuming to load and fire as my big toy revolver.

It had a pea shooter type short tube, a poor excuse for a barrel, which had to be unscrewed to remove it from the muzzle and then the pellet, a *cat slug,* had to be inserted before replacing it back into the main tube.

Then I had to cock the rifle like a pop gun, just to fire just one miserable weak pellet. It was neither powerful nor accurate but to me then, it was the best rifle in the world!

Having been on big-game safaris in the back garden at Camden Road hunting snails and doing not so accurate target shooting, using the half dozen or so brightly coloured feathered darts that came with it. I progressed to the more accurate, Beatles Wasted pellets, although these were considerably more expensive than the cat-slugs.

Of course, not knowing it at the time, I had found my one long-lasting sport in life, which I still hold dear to this day, that of rifle shooting!

I had a good couple of years' use from that silly little rifle and then, wanting something that was more accurate, more powerful, I progressed to a proper air rifle; one that was of a break-barrel type that could shoot both accurately and more than just a few feet.

It was not new, as we were far from being a well-off family although neither my mum nor dad ever let on to us kids. And not knowing where it came from, my dad presented me one day with this newer rifle. I was absolutely over the moon with it.

I never knew the make of it, just remember it had a hexagonal barrel and was certainly not a toy!

I also remember that I miss used it, just once, and my dad took it off me and locked it away for six months!

For the life of me, I cannot think back to what I must have done to get such a severe punishment? But punishment it certainly was and what seemed the longest six months of my childhood.

As childhood wanes, so along comes adolescence and my trusty air rifle was used less and less as I started to discover *girls* and so, the time for walks home after school, the odd invitation to a birthday party or meeting them at the end of the road now all took preference over me plinking at paper targets and tin cans in the back garden.

This was around 1964-65 and to remind you, back then there were no computers, video games, mobile phones, iPods, Walkman's, or even stereo sound.

In fact, it would be easier to list what there actually was, and it was not much. Maybe a trip to the cinema once a week, if I had *earned* some pocket money. A few hours at the local youth club, Marsh Street, and of course street corners to meet on and parks to walk through and sit in.

Anyhow, one of these girls, Margaret, whom I had a bit of a soft spot for, I began to walk home from school; and yes, I probably did carry her bag or books as that was then, *the* done thing as far more respect was shown to girls back then than now it seems.

We used to get back to her house where she and her

younger sister, Linda used to make me tea and toast and we used to just talk, that's all, just talk.

Her Mum would sometimes be there or come in from work or shopping and after an hour or so I would take my leave and walk home.

I remember one day though, whilst being there and enjoying the tea, toast and company of these two madcap young teenage girls, I heard what seemed to be the sound of, nothing short of what could have been an elephant entering the house by the front door.

There was banging and crashing that was virtually ignored by the two girls and then, appearing at the living room door stood this powerful-looking man, well over six feet tall, dressed in a green bomber jacket: carrying a vast amount of fishing paraphernalia. Their big brother Roy.

Now moved along the narrow passage, then through the small living room, out into the scullery and finally into the lean-to outside, Roy dumped his fishing tackle then returned to the living room to slump down in one of the two armchairs.

Ignoring me completely. He called out to the girls to bring him food and drink as though commanding mere peasants to come to his beck and call.

I, not even knowing that they had an elder brother, but now feeling awkward at being ignored, decided to take my leave.

On my next visit to the little house in Acacia Road, Roy was there again, this time just sitting watching TV and again there was something of an awkward silence between us, which was not surprising as I was just a kid of about fourteen at the time, and later found out that he was twenty-three years old.

Being as ever on my best behaviour, I only addressed

the girls, had my tea and toast and then as I was leaving, Roy, remaining focused on the TV and not looking in my direction, spoke to me. What made it really weird though was what he said.

"Have you got a gun?" he asked, not even taking his eyes off the TV. I, being taken aback replied saying,

"Well, yes, I have an old .177 air rifle."

"Good." he said, "bring it round Saturday and we'll go shooting if you like?"

I was stunned, to say the least. Yes, of course, it would have been my all-time wish for him to say such a thing, as I guess there was chemistry; at least on my part from the first instance, something like having the big brother I never had. But there had been no talk or mention of me even having a rifle or of shooting and that was very strange?

I could hardly wait for that Saturday to come. I had never shot anywhere outside of my own back yard and what were we to shoot? What gun did he have? Where were we going to go? My stomach was in knots when I knocked on the front door that Saturday carrying my silly little break-barrel air rifle.

At just five feet and some inches, Roy towered above me and had the build of an athlete or someone that works out in a gym. However, I soon found out that his build and fitness was due to him being in the Royal Marines and he was now home on leave.

Without too many words, hardly any, in fact, we went through the house in Acacia Road, out into the garden and I followed as Roy climbed over the fence at the end and looked back to see if I was following. I was, of course, and suddenly found myself in what I can only describe as a *jungle*.

The place was a mass of thorn bushes, nettles, trees, long grass and shrubs and soon I was afraid that I would be totally lost if I lost sight of my guide in such dense undergrowth, as I did not have a clue as to where I now was.

We walked for some distance, yards not miles, and then my first lesson in woodcraft started even before we had begun using our rifles, my silly little 177 rifle and his, .22 BSA Airsporter.

He started swearing and cussing at me about not walking quietly rather than crashing through the undergrowth! Yet all I was aware of, was trying to keep up with a man that took giant strides and not getting lost.

As he taught, I listened and learned. I learnt how to pick my footfalls and not step on twigs and other such matter, how to roll my foot, to feel the ground when it went down and so to walk in complete silence.

I wanted to learn more, but wondered, would he ever ask me out again after such clumsiness and stupidity from the start?

I honestly cannot even remember now if we fired our rifles that day or not, and if we did, I cannot remember at what? All I could think of was, "*Ask me out again, please, I'll be better next time.*"

Well, he did ask me out again, very many times, and I was better and kept on getting better, and with the swearing becoming less, I knew I must be improving.

Roy then taught me how to judge distances, he taught me about wind and elevation. About *hold over*, about controlling my breathing when taking a shot, about squeezing the trigger and not just pulling it, and I was loving every minute of it.

The land we were using, was now my training ground

for lessons in fieldcraft and belonged to Thames Water. I found out years later that it was known as a flood-field; a few acres set aside so that if London ever floods, this land and many other similar places, can be flooded to save the surrounding houses.

We rarely saw another person when in this urban jungle. It was so overgrown yet full of wildlife and when we did start shooting, we shot starlings and magpies and Roy with his more powerful rifle; shot the odd woodpigeon or two, although then, I was completely unaware of the eating of such delights, like pigeon pie or freshly fried pigeon breast, and I am now ashamed to say that virtually all of it was just left for fox food or to be eaten by rats.

3
FISHY TALES

I hated fishing, ever since I went with my junior school on just one of a couple of day trips to the late and great naturalist, Fred Speakmans` forest schoolhouse in High Beech, Epping.

It was the sight and feel of the wriggly worms and crawling maggots I detested, and I remember taking the maggots on this school trip in a jam-jar, sitting well away from the rest of the kids, then allowing a few maggots to crawl out onto the ground, then pinning one down with tweezers, I could then hook it, and in such a way did not have to actually touch it!

The one thing I did love though on those couple of visits to Epping Forest and Fred Speakmans` school, was the smell of the forest, the damp undergrowth, the dappled sunlight through the tree canopy, the leaf mould and even now, smelling that takes me back to my childhood.

Cold wet worms I hated with a passion and had quite a phobia of them ever since my younger brother, Jeff used to throw them over the top of the door of the outside loo at Camden Road. Mind you, I was very young then, so when Roy asked me one day if I wanted to go fishing with him, I replied, as I always did, and said, "Yes."

The first place I remember going to with him was on the River Lea at Cheshunt. Soon getting bored with the fishing side of things though, yet still being as pleased as punch just being there with him, now being tired, I curled up under the hedge at the side of the towpath and was soon asleep.

It was at first light when I awoke, the sky was a steely grey, and it was raining a light drizzle.

At some time during the night, Roy had covered me with an old blanket that I did not even know he had been packing, and there he was, still sitting there on his fishing box with a keep net now full of fish.

Seeing that I had now woken, he returned the fish to the river, and we went to a local café that morning for some breakfast before making our way back to Walthamstow by train.

I remember whilst sitting in that café the song: *House of the Rising Sun* by, The Animals playing on the cafe`s radio.

We hardly ever paid to get anywhere, as far as I can remember and to get to Broxbourne or Cheshunt, we used to board the train without a ticket at the station in Lea Bridge Road, by just walking onto the platform then walking off at the other end ignoring anyone that might call after us.

On the way back, we again just walked into the station, caught the train and then as it slowed to almost walking pace when crossing Walthamstow Marshes and *The Walthamstow Curve*, on more than one occasion, we just opened the door, threw our stuff out and then jumped off after it down the embankment, then hiked home across the marshes.

They say ignorance is no defence in the eyes of the law, but I was truly ignorant in some matters, with no thought of having to have a fishing licence or having to have permission to shoot on land. Although being fair, things were not as they are today and in comparison, it was like living in a completely different world back then.

During that first summer, of 1964, I had met very few of Roy's friends and just a couple of his girlfriends, but as the year passed and winter approached, thinking one day we were going to go over the *jungle* to shoot. I was pleasantly surprised to find that we walked through this no man's land, then across the rear of St James` Park (Walthamstow) and then on to the marshes and then, still further onto Walthamstow Reservoirs.

We then climbed the concrete fence that encircled it, and again, I was about to discover a whole new world, one of, ducks, vast open space, water, and of peace, quiet and tranquillity.

We walked and walked and then, in the near distance, I saw what looked to be snow or something snow-like, coming in small flurries over the top of one part of the banking.

We climbed the slope and there on the far side was, Ginger, a skinny guy with hair as red as a sunset, sitting there on the grass plucking pigeons and smiling from ear to ear.

From the welcome, it was obvious he and Roy knew each other, and laughter, banter and talk ensued. Ginger had pigeon feathers in his red hair, and this is what I had taken to be snowflakes.

At his feet he had these little naked birds; that he had

shot, about half a dozen of them with his 12-gauge shotgun that lay next to him and was truly pleased with his bag.

I am guessing that Ginger was about the same age as Roy and during the weeks that followed, I came to meet a whole bunch of guys that were, or seemed to be, his friends that he had never mentioned before.

They all seemed to be gentle rogues, but I was young, naïve and very impressionable being so young, that I was just taken in by them and all that went with them.

They might well have been the biggest crooks in the East End for all I knew, but I never even thought of things like that back then, and probably would not have cared even if they had been.

Shooting over the *ressers,* as they were known to us, suddenly became quite a Sunday ritual and although I never owned a shotgun at that time, I was upgraded and allowed to now carry and use, Roy's air rifle, his BSA Airsporter for taking sitting pigeon and general plinking.

I remember how heavy it weighed at the time and wondered just how he could carry such a thing all day but again, I was young and slight of build in comparison.

Saying that times were far different then is no exaggeration; we used to carry an air rifle and a shotgun along several side roads and a couple of lanes in broad daylight, not in slips or cases and then onto Walthamstow Reservoirs or Walthamstow Marshes to shoot the pigeon that came off the islands at first light. One could not imagine ever doing that nowadays without helicopters suddenly hovering in the sky and armed police and police cars screaming all over the place.

The *marsh shooters* banged away for a good couple of hours and then we went to the Woodman Café aka earlier, Nan`s Cafe` by the Lea Marina, for a big Sunday fry up breakfast or big bacon butties; again. With guns and cartridge belts strewn all over the tables and wet dogs and muddy Wellington boots, no one ever complained, no police were ever called, and no trouble was ever had. I lived for and loved those Sunday mornings.

One winters` morning, I remember, I had walked alone down and out onto the marshes; I am guessing here that Roy must have been away at sea.

It was cold yet dry and so quiet I could hear the tall dead reeds clicking and rattling together in the wind, making a hollow sound and as I stood and looked out across the brown winter wasteland, I could see no one.

I remember feeling terrible, quite lost and alone in fact, as I looked forward so much to those mornings, just seeing and being with the other guys, the marsh shooters. Being around them on the marsh and in the café. I felt my spirits just fall away and then, as a single lone pigeon came off East Warwick reservoir heading full tilt out over the marsh, so I heard, BANG! BANG! BANG!; and more followed. There must have been close to thirty shots put up at this one bird from the shooters from all over the marsh and I suddenly felt uplifted, my spirits rising high, and I could not wait to see the guys again.

They were a motley bunch that's for sure. All of various ages, backgrounds and attire, but I thought them the greatest guys to be around.

There was Black Powder Pete, who only ever used cheap Russian black powder cartridges. You always knew exactly where he was on the marsh, as when he fired his gun a great cloud of white smoke could be seen rising from the grasses.

There was Chrissy Bland, one of the nicest guys you could ever wish to meet and Albie Chalice, who could hardly see a hand in front of his face but could see pigeon and tell you whether they were *streeters* or *woodies* a mile away and then drop them effortlessly when in range.

Then there was big Jimmy Bradshaw, who, both short and stocky, carried a four-bore muzzleloader no less, and who I saw take out two ducks with one shot at the end of West Warwick one Sunday.

I first saw the flash from that beast of a gun, which emitted a flame about fifteen feet long, shortly followed by a boom that sounded like thunder rolling across the sky. Then many minutes later, he returned to the marina end of the reservoirs, smiling, holding a pair of shot mallard. He once offered his gun for Roy to shoot I remember but for all his size, Roy just smiled and declined.

There was `Yogi`, a young good-looking guy, who was so tight or perhaps just hard up? That turned up, sometimes, with just one shell in his cartridge belt and then leached cartridges off everyone else. His forte was, that he could throw a Bowie style knife into a tree from easily twenty paces and make it stick every time.

Then there was old Bill Reilly, his party piece was to be able to throw an old pre-decimal penny in the air and shoot it with an air rifle, hitting his mark four out of five times! He went on to shoot black powder shotguns and win many trophies.

I used to see Bill many times up at my local gun shop in later years, he was still as wild and never wore socks, no matter what the weather, but alas since starting this book he has since passed away like so many of them now have. Gone to that great hunting ground in the sky. But what a great bunch they were, the likes of which will never be seen again, each a character, each with a story, each a legend in his own right.

Through Roy, I was accepted by this mixed wild bunch from day one and was soon utilised by them to whistle in woodpigeons that left the islands on the *ressers*.

This meant I used to be in a forward position on the far side, the waterside, of the banking with the guns behind me in hiding and as the pigeons came closer; with me not moving a muscle, I whistled first slow, then faster and the men (guns) then knew that they could raise their heads above the parapet (top of the embankment) and blast away before the birds had a chance to veer off.

Still only having Roy's Airsporter I could not, of course, shoot birds in flight, even though I have downed two in my life since, using a single-shot air rifle, I was though, allowed to finish off any that were *walkers* and had only been pricked by the odd shotgun pellet or two.

The shotguns that these guys used were something to behold, and probably far more dangerous than the men behind them. Many of them were damaged in some way, taped up with Gaffer tape around the stock, or were so ill-fitting that they rattled and were loose at the breach.

I think it was Chrissy Bland, that one day had the ventilated rib of his old side by side double, roll up and look like a coiled spring at the end of his barrel and although none of the guns actually blew up, none that I saw anyway, it would not have surprised me to hear of it.

The reason for these guns being in this condition was simple. If the police ever did turn up, then the gun, or *gas pipe,* as they sometimes called them, would be flung into the reservoir and you cannot charge someone for shooting on a reservoir if they have not got a gun.

I never saw the police on the marshes, and they must have known of our existence and surely heard us on those Sunday mornings with the sound of so many shots reverberating and echoing up Springfield Park and into Clapton and Stamford Hill, and to catch us would not have been that hard.

We used to regularly meet up, fire a few shots off at pigeons, have breakfast before going home. I like to think that there was an understanding at the time, a kind of respect even and something that is very much lost in today's world.

There used to be a waterboard patrolman we called Johnny Liar, that walked the *ressers* with a gummy old Alsatian dog.

"Alright lads," he would say, if he got close enough, "we have the reservoirs surrounded so you might as well give up now."

"Okay Johnny," we would reply, "we're just off now anyway." And would then simply walk away. No lip, no backchat, or threats. After all, he was only doing the job he was paid to do and even though he had made this ridiculous statement about the reservoirs being surrounded. Which, in reality, an entire army could not do, we still respected him enough for the challenge he made, and we never caused him grief or hardship. They were good days that will never ever come back and are now lost to history.

With no actual powers of arrest, the waterboard men were never going to gain anything, but I do have a friend who some years later was a tad unlucky, as he was shooting over Number 5 one Sunday afternoon by himself, with two bird watchers in the distance: a man and a boy. Walking up to the man, he simply asked the time, and the man casually looked at his watch and replied,

"It's a quarter to four and you're nicked!" It turned out the bird watcher was a policeman with his son. The fine was ten pounds, a considerable amount then, but over the years the story has paid for itself many times over.

One day, I was with Roy, and Keith Sullivan, a very long-time school friend of mine, that in turn, I had been introduced to both Roy and shooting.

On this particular morning over the *ressers*, having been out, but with nothing about, we were walking the banking, doing no harm, when suddenly we saw two waterboard men at a distance, dressed similar to police in dark peaked caps and long, almost trench-like heavy coats. coming towards us. We decided, rather than face them and get into any kind of confrontation, to turn and just walk away.

Looking over our shoulder we then saw that they were now trotting after us, so we picked up the pace and started to trot ourselves. They then began to pick up speed and were now running!

"These must be young bucks out for the chase?" I am thinking and never being much of an athlete where running is concerned, I started to get a bit anxious that they might even actually catch me.

"Let's split up?" one of us suggested, and so we did, thinking that two cannot catch three. It made little difference though, as I still had one chasing me and now my mouth was feeling dry, and I was beginning to think that I too, might end up with a ten-pound fine and a meeting in front of the local Beak. I probably would have too, but after another couple of hundred yards the waterboard man chasing me, gave up the chase and taking his hat off I saw him throw it to the ground in temper and frustration.

I thought about it afterwards, running in one of those heavyweight rubberised long raincoats must have been hell for the guy, but nonetheless, I was still glad to have escaped. None of us was caught that day and the waterboard men got some exercise to boot, so all was well in the end.

As the seasons passed, Roy and I fished the *ressers* as well as shot them and I did finally find fishing something of a sport but have never really had the same passion for it as I have for shooting.

We fished for pike in the winter and bream and perch in the warmer months and I remember us catching some nice perch one morning and cooking them, then and there, over an open fire right at the water's edge; they were both crispy and delicious.

We once baited a corner of reservoir number 5 for a week with bread, just walking there each evening throwing in lots of stale bread, and then on the chosen night, fished it for bream.

We pulled out fish after fish all night long and all good sizes too, but bream never really put up much of a fight even though they look as though they could and should.

I took one home to see what it tasted like but found it bland even though it had chunky flesh like that of cod.

One of the most exciting fishing forays we ever had, was on a freezing cold winter's night with snow on the ground when we fished for pike.

It had been a well-planned trip, so we had a flask of

black coffee, plenty of smokes, some sandwiches and were well wrapped up but it was still so very cold.

Roy and I settled down with just a couple of rods out on East Warwick and were using herring as dead bait. The cold wind coming over the dark waters was bitter, and I remember Roy kept asking me to make him roll-ups (cigarettes) which I did the best I could with frozen fingers.

After a while, we suddenly heard an enormous splash, almost as though someone had thrown a brick into the water. Then, after a minute or so of silence, we heard it again and again.

This repeated itself over and over, the splashing sounding louder and ever closer. Finally, startling me, it was just below Roy's rod tip. The water plumed, there was a massive spray and Roy sprang to his feet and made a grab for the landing net. Shouting orders for me to get a torch he ran to the edge of the water where I saw him swing the net like a golf club.

What I saw next was almost beyond belief. Roy had scooped the pike up into the net and it was now half in and half out as the landing nets` handle bent and the giant fish was lifted high into the air.

Then, with a sudden flick of its muscular body, the huge fish snapped the net at the folding joint as though it was a twig and sailed back into the dark waters like a leaping salmon.

After some moments of eerie silence, the splashing began all over again as the pike started a second tour close to the margins; around the massive reservoir, it toured, splash followed by silence as it cruised the water's edge.

It was now a matter of some urgently needed repair

work on the crippled folding landing net as we both tried to bind it up at the centre hinged joint using some found wax baling twine.

It took a couple of hours for the predatory fish to complete a second circuit around the margins, but this time Roy was ready for it, almost guessing where it would come splashing and crashing at the water's edge.

Once more, it did, Roy swung, the fish was again in the net, then it flipped just as before, and the net yet again collapsed as the string gave way.

The net now looked like a giant hook or `?`, with its netting hanging loose and useless from the rear curved part of it, but that did not seem to bother Roy who scooped at the beast yet again and this time managed to hook the jointed part of the net into the pike's gills.

The pole began to bend once more, Roy heaved, and the fish again rose into the air, this time over his left shoulder and landed with a heavy sounding wet thump on the concrete sloping shelf that was the banking of East Warwick.

I remember Roy literally then pouncing on the fish, pinning it down with his knees, before getting his lock knife out and plunging it deep into the top of its head.

It was indeed a monster of the deep and no, me, shaking with excitement rather than the cold we spoke of ways of getting this thing weighed?

I had only one suggestion come to mind, that of the corner shop, Bennetts, across from where I lived at the junction of Camden and Arkley Road.

It was owned and run by Sid Bennett, always *Mr Bennett* to me, and he had a yard out the back where he had potato scales for weighing bags of spuds.

That was good enough for Roy, so we packed up the tackle and set off on the long walk home to my place.

It was past two in the morning when we knocked up Mr Bennett, and he came to the side door of his shop in pyjamas and slippers wearing a plaid dressing gown.

I first apologised, more than once, for getting him out of bed at this ungodly hour on a winter`s night whilst Roy, playing it dumb just stood back and stayed quiet.

I explained that it would be good of him if he could see his way clear just to let us weigh this fish on his potato scales in his backyard?

Now, whether it was curiosity on his part that made him say yes, or he may have decided it was just the quickest way to get rid of us; or maybe even that he had known me and my family that lived almost opposite for so many years but anyhow, Mr Bennett agreed, as it was an enormous fish, and within a few minutes and in the freezing cold of a midwinter's night we three weighed the pike as best we could to find it just under 30 pounds, a true monster of Walthamstow reservoirs.

I am not sure whether we ate that one, but we did eat others and their taste varied depending on where we had caught them. Those that came from muddy bottom rivers tended to be horrible and earthy tasting, whereas those that came off gravel bottom rivers tasted very good, and the Jewish community of Stamford Hill used to pay good money for pike.

In years since, I have caught plenty of other pike, my personal best being 12 pounds on the river Lea, (Lee) near Broxbourne, but nothing anywhere near like that beast we caught on that winters` night over East Warwick.

4
MAN TRAPS, THE 'BRUDDERS' AND A CLOSE CALL

The flood field or jungle, where Roy had first introduced me to fieldcraft had something of a chequered history as I discovered some years later, and at one time had supposedly been the site of a hospital. Typhoid, I think?

Anyway, walking through the tall grasses, one would come across, mostly by tripping over them, stumpy wrought iron railings that looked as though they separated graves of those that had died there and were buried in the grounds. Although these may well have just been where allotment plot holders had used something to separate their plots at some time or another in previous, forgotten years. Other quite lethal obstacles were also to be found, like the 40-gallon oil drums that had had their tops and bottoms cut away and then had been sunk deep into the ground, one on top of the other and allowed to fill with water, thereby making them into deep hidden wells.

The purpose of these, obviously being a way of

providing a water supply to the people that worked the plots. Had there, of course, been allotments there many years before? Indeed, allotments were just on the other side of a small and dirty brook that divided this field from allotments that still exist to this day.

One of Roy's friends, Al Simon, had a younger brother Jeff, who I later bought my very first shotgun from had been over the flood field with a friend of his on a day when I had been over there alone.

I had seen him hobbling in the distance, being helped along by a friend and I also saw that he was in a bad way. It turned out that he had fallen into one of these hidden wells and the rusted and jagged sides of this potential mantrap had caught him under each arm as he fell into it. His clothes were shredded from his waist to his armpits, and he was covered in blood, a real mess.

From then on, although by now I knew where all these pitfalls were, I took to carrying smoke pellets; the type that gas fitters or plumbers use to seek out leaky pipes, just in case I had the same misfortune and needed to somehow attract attention.

Mobile phones had not been invented then and one could have shouted all day long and would never have been heard or seen in this patch of dense wasteland.

The flood field ran between the allotments and an open-air, rifle range that was on Walthamstow Council property, and was used by the Ensign Rifle Club, a club that had been around for some forty years and had its origins in the Ensign Camera Company, that produced cameras like the Kodak Brownie Box camera.

At the furthest end of this rifle range, which was well over a hundred yards long, and ending in a steep bank or hill, stood a man-made miniature mountain known locally to kids as Ash Mountain.

This was some forty to fifty high and had been created over very many years by the Council bin men emptying the hot ashes that had been collected from the coal-fired houses in Walthamstow, and even though for years no hot embers had been added to this tip, it still steamed and smoked in the winter as if it were alive like some small volcano.

It was full of rats when we, Roy and myself first began shooting over there and we would sometimes come across one or two lying on the surface that had been burned, I am guessing, by being somehow caught within this smouldering hilltop.

My dad told me once of a schoolboy at his school, that was not the brightest of lads, that made a hideout in the side of Ash Mountain and lived there for a while. He had a nickname like Scooby or something.

The view from the top of Ash Mountain was spectacular, and one could see over to St. James` Park and beyond to Walthamstow Marshes in one direction and in the other, the spire of St Saviours Church in Markhouse Road, and The Lighthouse Church, which really was and is today, a lighthouse, and not the only landlocked lighthouse in London.

The flood field was cleared many years ago now and no longer looks like the jungle it once was. Housing has also been built close to it and for all I know, may well be all housing now. Although I did hear that due to the heavy metal content of the area, this caused something of a problem where planning was concerned.

The allotments, which I had shot over illegally for years, ran alongside the jungle and many years later, having served a few years in the army, I gained permission from the Allotment Association, to shoot there legally and later became known as *pigeon man*.

One Sunday morning, still using an air rifle at the time, I took out a woodpigeon sitting at the top of a high tree and seeing it fall dead to the ground, walked over to pick it up only to find that it had gone? A little way off was a black guy tending his vegetables, so I went up to him asking if he had seen the bird fall, which he must have, being that close to the base of the tree.

"No man, I ain`t seen nutink!" he replied and continued scratching away at the ground with a hoe.

I did a 360-degree turn and picked up the blood trail, following it directly to his allotment shed and could only laugh, to think that he had poached and robbed me of my planned breakfast of pan-fried woodpigeon!

On another occasion, having shot a *woodie* the day before and taking it home, I had removed the breasts and returned the following evening with just the feathered carcase to use as a decoy. I set it out on one of the plots, propping its head up using a `Y` shaped twig then hid behind a shed in wait of another bird coming down on the crops. I did not have to wait long, and one soon did and so I whacked it, killing it stone dead.

Picking it up, I saw this old black feller tending his crops and we got into a conversation about eating pigeons, and so I then offered him the newly shot bird, telling him how to take off the breasts as there was not much else of any use on the creature, but he insisted that the carcase of the other one would be fine.

I told him over and over, that there was nothing on it, as I had removed the meat the previous day! In the end, I plucked the newly shot bird, gave that to him and the other one minus its breast meat and said he could get a half-decent stew from the two birds.

He then offered me a drink of whiskey from a bottle he kept in his shed, and we talked some more until it was almost dark and were finally the last to leave.

"Well, brudder," he sighed, "I got to be going now as I got to get me pills!"

"Pills?" I questioned,

"Where are you going to get pills from at this time of night? There are no chemists open."

"From de off-license man!" he answered with a laugh. What he meant was Pilsner beer!

———

Another time I was over the allotments, on a Sunday morning and having shot a few pigeons, I was just on my way out at about ten in the morning when some *brothers* were sitting around drinking and laughing. Seeing me, they invited me to join them. Well, one drink led to another and in the end, having sat there for well over an hour, I was well and truly tipsy by the time I left them but had had a great time. It was a good job I lived only walking distance away too, as I was in no way fit to drive.

One winter's morning, I was creeping about the allotments as I had now been issued a key to let myself in and out and standing by the side of one of the sheds, I began to hear a rustling sound.

I thought at first it might well be a rat scratching about, but it went on and on and I started to feel a bit apprehensive. I began to step back slowly and got myself at the side of another shed and waited. After a while, and to my surprise a black guy came out of the shed where the rustling sounds had come from fully dressed in a grey suit and tie carrying a briefcase and casually walked off out of the allotments as bold as you like.

When he had gone, I moved to the shed he had come from and peering through the grimy window saw that inside he had a made-up single bed, a mirror on the wall and an oil lamp on a small table. The guy was obviously living there, and I got to thinking that it's not such a bad place to live really. He had shelter, peace and quiet, fresh water from the system that filled the troughs and fresh vegetables all around and what's more the yearly rent was only about £12.

Over the many years I shot on those allotments I discovered another three guys living in their sheds, so I guess if you multiplied that by the number of allotments in the whole of the country, there are an awful lot of single men living in sheds far away from the madding crowd.

———

The most dangerous adventure or episode, I had over those allotments, was on one very cold winter's morning in March. Having arrived as usual at just about first light. I began to walk the narrow pathways between the huts and sheds looking for pigeons feeding on whatever remained of any of the crops.

I had covered about three-quarters of the entire place and only seeing one other guy tending to something or other outside his little hut, just acknowledged him with a nod of my head. Shortly after this and without notice, or even time to blink, I heard what sounded like a firework, a rocket to be more precise, going off but in reverse if that makes sense? The sound was a kind of whooshing noise immediately followed by a thump that literally shook the ground around me!

Something had come hurtling out of the cold clear blue sky, and seeing just a white flash, something had passed me at terrific speed, just missing me and a shed, almost completely burying itself in the frozen ground no more than ten paces from where I stood!

My immediate thought was it must have been a meteorite, and I almost expected to see smoke rising from the ground, but on approaching it, I now clearly saw that the object embedded in the frozen soil, was that of a big block of ice.

I then quite naively, bent to pick it up only to find it to be held solid, so finding an old piece of angle iron, I proceeded to lever this *thing* from the ground. Then finding an old carrier bag, I put this block of ice into it, as I thought no one would ever believe me unless they saw it with their own eyes and so proceeded to take it home.

It virtually filled the bag and weighed, I estimated about ten pounds. It all clicked into place then that this had not come from another planet, but rather a plane overhead.

Once home, I put it in the garden and took photos of it, comparing its size with that of a house brick. Then the next day, Monday, I contacted the Civil Aviation Authority.

Having noted roughly, the time, of this icefall and that there were three planes overhead on that clear morning. Then thinking of the ice falling from the sky, I gave the CAA the colours of their livery and the time and direction in which they had been flying, I still got nowhere with any enquires and all I had was a story for family and friends.

It would have been one hell of a mystery though had it hit and killed me, as could you imagine the police looking for a killer that would never have existed as in time the ice would have melted leaving no trace.

The CAA did ask me though, what colour the ice was, blue or white? As apparently, white ice comes from the plane's drinking water supply valve; blue ice comes from the toilet system. And the way this happens is when the plane reduces altitude and the water, having frozen onto the outside of the plane at a greater height, suddenly just falls off as it reaches lower altitude and warms slightly.

This is far more common than people are aware of and having shown this block of potential killer ice to a neighbour, he came over to me some weeks later and showed me an article in the Times Newspaper, where similar ice falls had smashed through conservatory roofs almost killing people, especially near Kew Gardens, as planes came into land at Heathrow Airport. I had been extremely lucky that day as I ticked another one of my nine lives from the list.

5
CUT TO THE CHASE

Both Walthamstow Marshes and the chain of reservoirs that run from Chingford in the north to the river Lea (Lee) and Walthamstow in the south are abundant with many kinds of wildlife.

The marshes are now a conservation area, known as Walthamstow Wetlands and have a boardwalk in part crossing them so that people can walk across and observe the many types of butterflies in the summer as well as the many plants, wildflowers, sedges and grasses. The reservoirs are also home to many species of wildfowl and other birds as well as the millions of gallons of water that Londoners rely on.

Some of the reservoirs have islands in the centre of them and these act as roosting places for herons, pigeons, crows and an array of various ducks and geese.

The reservoirs have changed though since I was young and used to walk them, for one can now fish them on a day ticket, and some are stocked with trout and as well as holding all the more common types of course fish like perch, bream, pike, and roach.

Had I been born ten years earlier, no doubt I would have ventured over the then, monstrous reservoir known as The Racecourse, where now, the pumping station and filter beds stand.

This vast expanse of water contained no less than four islands and the older guys that I found myself hanging about with related and told stories of them spending whole weekends on these islands having boated out to them and there lived like Huckleberry Finn or Tom Sawyer; fishing and eating all they caught in the way of fish and birds.

A couple of these guys, *borrowed* a dingy from the marina once and taking it to The Racecourse, paddled it out there where it sank! Just how they gained the attention of the waterboard men, I never did find out, probably by lighting a fire, but they were rescued and made a story in the local paper. It's hard to believe that all this went on just a few short miles from the City of London, but it did.

When I upgraded from an air rifle to a shotgun, the first one I bought was known as a garden gun, which is just 9mm in calibre. They are far from powerful, having an effective range of maybe ten to fifteen yards and primarily used against something like rats in a barn.

The one I had I bought I got off Jeff Simons, and was of German manufacture, an Anschutz, and was a single shot bolt action. Sometime during its life, it had what looked to be a choke of sorts welded to the muzzle which made it look as if it furnished a silencer, and this added about another 4 inches to the barrel length. I, being young, thought this made it look great as I always had a liking for the odd and the slightly different.

Anyway, having bought this shotgun and the legal license that was then available from the local post office for just 10 shillings and 6 pence in old money (55p today) I was as happy as happy could be.

One of the features of these garden guns, besides the fact that one would be hard-pressed to shoot pigeons in flight with them, is that there were only two types of cartridges available for them.

The first a chrome-coloured shell about an inch and half long with a yellow cardboard cap in its end to hold in the tiny number 7 or 8 shot, and the second made by Eley, was a black powder crimped green paper shell, with a copper cap that held the priming cap. When this was fired, the whole of the paper cartridge case went down the barrel along with the shot and exuded from the muzzle in a cloud of smoke and burning paper leaving only the small copper cap to be ejected when the bolt was operated.

This was by far my favourite shell to use as it looked impressive when fired but being a black powder cartridge, I had to boil out the barrel when cleaning the gun to remove the gunk and residue the cartridge had left behind.

With no rats in barns to shoot, I still found a good use for this little garden gun and that was to remove the yellow cardboard cap of the unnamed chromed shells, empty out the tiny shot and replace this with .22 air rifle pellets, of which when crushed with pliers, I could get six or seven inside the casing. I then could either take out a sitting pigeon in a tree if able to get close enough or at night I would go over the reservoirs and creep up on the surface feeding mallards in the corner or close to the edge and pop off one of these ducks before they all took flight.

The gun only made the sound of a .22 rifle; a crack

sound and nothing like the big bang of say a 12-bore shotgun.

Having no tidal flow on the reservoirs it was then just a matter of waiting for the wind to blow the dead bird close enough to the water's edge before retrieving it and going home with the spoils of the night.

I used to go over the reservoirs at about the same time all my mates were coming home after a night down at the pub and my mum especially thought, I was maybe not quite right, or even weird in my nocturnal habits.

I did not care though as I thought, in fact, knew, I was having far more fun than anyone else and bringing home a duck or two at the weekend was always a bonus.

———

However, one night, was particularly unforgettable as I had gone out, walked the fifteen minutes or so from Camden Road to Coppermill Lane, then having climbed over the concrete fence into the reservoirs found myself at the corner of number 5.

The night was still and calm and I could hear, in the distance, the constant drone and humming of the traffic along the surrounding main roads. It was this distant humming sound that made me love the reservoirs for its solitude and peacefulness.

Ducks quacked and squabbled and chirped depending on the breed and I listened for the distinctive grating Yak! Yak! Yak! Yak! call of a mallard to pinpoint its position. I then moved around the base of the steep embankment on the grass side before crawling up the slope to peer over the top.

On this night, I did just that and saw by the ambient

reflected light in the sky, four or five mallards pecking away at the surface weed in the corner.

With my heart racing a little faster than normal and the adrenaline beginning to flow I slowly, very slowly, slid my gun into position, eased off the safety, took aim and fired!

Crack went the gun and daylight became the scene as lights came on piercing the night from three different positions! Police!

Whether it was just a fluke; a coincidence, or whether I had just become too complacent, too much a creature of habit and gone over there maybe once too often, or too often on the same night of the week I will never know. But what I did know and was sure about, was that these coppers meant business and had been in wait for me.

A police car with its lights on full beam was parked by the main gate in Sandy Alley, the continuation of Coppermill Lane and two policemen on Noddy bikes, (Velocette motorbikes) had turned their lights on and were now making their way towards me from two different directions, around the top of the reservoir along the wide flat top of the banking.

Now a well-kept cut grass, a reservoir is not the best place in which to find a hiding place and having slid down the embankment, forgetting about whether I had a dead duck to collect, I now began to run for all I was worth around the base of number 5 and away from where I had entered at the end of Coppermill Lane.

Finding myself in a kind of gully with the banking rising on my left and a concrete fence on my right that even if I had scaled it, only lead to a long drop and the big concrete overflow canal. I returned, once more, scrambling up the side of the embankment to see just where and how sincere these coppers on motorbikes were in finding me.

Oh, they were sincere alright and were now riding in a figure of eight around number 5 and would be soon on me.

Now, running towards The Bar, the narrow strip of land that separates reservoirs 5 from 4, then along the eastern side of number 4, towards the railway lines, that pass alongside and parallel to Forest Road. I can remember singing to myself, under strained breath the Dave Clark song: *Catch Us If You Can.*

I was drenched in sweat, my mouth feeling as dry as a bone, but I was making ground, although not nearly as fast as the Noddy bikes were. Then, as though someone was looking out for me, I suddenly saw it; a pylon, and the long grass beneath it that the mowers had been unable to reach.

Pausing at the edge of the tall grass, I literally dived headfirst into it trying not to make an entry path.

Then pulling, the tall blades up around me as fast and as best I could, both saw and heard the motorbikes coming close to where I was laying. Holding my breath in the undergrowth I was just feet in front of them.

Their lights were now shining right across me and to both left and right; their radios were crackling with police chatter, and I thought to myself, how can they not have seen me? But see me they did not, and away they went again touring the reservoirs.

I breathed a sigh of relief, but I was not out of the woods (or grass) yet.

For two and a half hours those policemen went round and round searching for me and passed me more than once.

Finally, when they were at the furthest point distant from my hiding place and had given me time to think of an escape route. I broke cover and ran for all I was worth towards the railway. Breathlessly crossing the lines, and then climbing a four-foot wall on the reservoir side, I then dropped ten or twelve feet to the pavement on the other side, into Forest Road not far from the pub, The Ferry Boat Inn.

Breathless, hot, sweating and thirsty, I crossed the road to the same side as the pub, still with my 9mm shotgun in hand and waited for and caught, a bus home.

Just how long the police kept up their search for me I never knew, but it had been an exciting adventure, with this little piggy smiling all the way home.

6

CRAZY KIDS AND GUNS

It is probably hard to believe now, but back in the 1960s, one could buy a shotgun via a mail-order company; one could just pick them out of a catalogue.

No Internet then, and both I and my friend, Steve that lived just two doors away, bought guns from a catalogue company like this. Both were single barrel 12-bores called Cooey`s. They were cheap and just about functional but at the time we thought they were great.

Now, having a 12-bore shotgun meant that I could at least *try* and shoot birds in flight, although I was never much good at it. Where I did have some use to the other, older guys though that I hung about with over the reservoirs, was that I could now *scare* the pigeons towards them.

I have already mentioned, there are islands over the reservoirs that are roosting places for many birds, pigeons being just one kind. So, being shown by Roy how to make what was known as string shot and solids, I was duly stationed off at an angle to the group of Sunday morning shooters and to give the pigeons a wake-up call, when the men were in position, I fired one or two solids out over the waters towards the island.

The sound was something to behold as the blast of a 12-bore early on a quiet morning anywhere would be enough to shake anyone out of bed, but to fire a 12-bore over the *ressers* at first light was truly awesome and almost immediately, sometimes hundreds of pigeons would leave the island all at once, take to the sky and fly hard and fast and hopefully, towards the waiting guns lined up along the banking.

The solid was a cartridge made by un-crimping the end of the then cardboard, shotgun shell pouring out the lead shot into a container; then using a candle the wax dripped into the shell case as the lead shot was also gently poured back in. The candle wax then quickly set and so held all the shot together in the casing, so when fired, instead of spreading into the pattern it was meant to, it remained held solid, or pretty much so, for a much greater distance before breaking up.

This was not meant for shooting pigeons of course, and I seriously doubt that one would hit a bird in flight with one of these altered cartridges, but they certainly did the job of scaring the birds into flight and sometimes I could hear the shot crashing through the trees on the island which was a considerable distance away.

The other made-up shot was string shot. This was meant for taking out birds in flight, primarily geese, and again, the sound of a gun firing string shot can be awesome to hear.

To create string shot, one does as before. Opens the crimped end of the 12 gauge shell, pours out the loose shot and has ready a length of fishing line with fishing weights pinched onto it at short intervals of say, half an inch.

This is then fed into the empty shell casing and coiled up and the crimp closed. When the shell is fired the string of lead shot spins much like a bolero towards the desired target and if it happens to be a goose and hits it right it has a devastating effect, sometimes even decapitating the bird in flight.

The sound it makes when fired can be anything from a humming noise to a harsh screaming whistle. Both these types of shells when constructed were marked as to what they were and kept separate from normal 12-gauge ammunition.

———

Yes, I was young and sometimes silly, but not as crazy as of all people, a neighbour and the son of a policeman, Billy, who was next door to where I did in Camden Road when the waste ground there had six purpose-built police flats erected on it.

I became friendly with two of the copper's sons; Peter Cornwall, who went to the same school as me, and Billy, (*Welshie*) who was a good-looking kid I remember and a couple of years younger than me but was a complete nutcase.

Welshie, found the reservoirs and marsh poaching life all by himself with no need of any introduction from me, and as far as handmade ammunition went?

Well, I met him one Sunday morning over the marshes, just walking around aimlessly with a side by side 12 gauge.

We got to talking and he suddenly said, "Look at

this." And then commenced shooting both barrels of his side-by-side at a slatted concrete fence that was about an inch and a half thick from just a few yards away. The sound was terrific, as was the damage to the fence as a big hole now appeared in it.

"What the hell are you using?" I asked.

"Marbles!" He replied, smiling his slightly crooked maniacal smile.

Yes, he had home loaded glass marbles. I thought at the time, he had maybe lost his *marbles*, and this was confirmed sometime later when I saw him returning home one day from the reservoirs, walking along the road wearing a wet suit and carrying a spear gun with a huge eel still squirming on the tri-pronged spear over his back.

Crazy Billy, I often wondered whatever happened to him?

———

Steve Hume never really kept up with shooting and hunting after his younger days, but when he did have his shotgun, a single barrel like mine, we used to go over the marshes and flood field now and then together.

I remember one very windy Sunday morning we had returned home, empty-handed of course, to Camden Road. When we saw a whole bunch of neighbours out, looking up at another neighbour's rooftop.

Crossing the road, we soon saw what they were looking at. One of the neighbours was a pigeon fancier and kept racing pigeons in his back garden.

It seemed that one of his better birds had been returning to the loft when a sudden gust of wind had blown the poor thing downward and now, there it was, impaled and flapping helplessly with about 2 feet of what looked to be a vertical ariel through its body.

It did not take much back for a crowd of neighbours to gather back then, and there they were, women wearing turbans and aprons, arms folded across their big bosoms, some with cigarettes dangling from their lips; just yards up Arkley Road and not far from old Sid Bennett`s corner shop.

There were a few men there also and between them, all with advice to give.

"Can`t someone get a ladder from somewhere and help the poor thing?"

"You`ll need a crawling board as well to get up to the roof and the chimney stack."

"It`ll be dead anyway soon, I reckon!"

"Best just wring its neck!"

Came the calls from those that were gathered.

Steve and I were now standing there, seeing and hearing all this and I stepped forward.

"I can end its suffering with this?" I said, touching my gun in its slip.

The guy who owned the bird just ignored me as did the rest of the crowd and some went away only to return shortly afterwards with a triple wooden ladder and a couple of the men helped the pigeon`s owner get it up to the chimney stack and the skewered bird.

Precariously climbing the stack and grabbing the pigeon, the guy then had to slide it back up and off the rod that had speared it.

Even then the whole thing seemed ridiculous, for even if the bird had survived it would never have raced again. But no, it died soon after the rescue attempt and the guy that had risked his own neck for the sake of his racing pigeon was lucky not to have been blown off the roof and killed.

———

It is strange though what people will do for their pets and there have been countless tales of people drowning trying to save their dogs for instance.

Apparently, as I was not there at the time to witness it, short-sighted Albie Chalice shot his own dog one day over the reservoirs.

He had a little mongrel named Nigger and, on this day, as he had done many times before, he had grabbed it by the scruff of the neck and tossed it over the concrete fence and was just about to climb over after it, when the silly dog ran back through the fence but further down. Albie, thinking it was a rat or something just fired his gun instinctively and peppered his own dog. I heard that he spent hours picking out lead shot from it, but it did survive.

7
NEW BEGINNINGS FOR ALL

My shooting forays with Roy were not only confined to the local reservoirs, marshes and flood field, or jungle.

I remember once going to a rough shoot somewhere near the east coast and shooting rabbits in an empty quarry. That was a fun day, banging the rabbits as they ran from place to place beneath small steel dump trucks, that was on an old narrow-gauge railway line.

The day was hot and dry, I remember, and the shot kicked up the dust in great clouds as it peppered the ground looking like something from a Spaghetti Western film.

It was on that day that I saw my very first wild fox. I was sixteen, and how times have changed. Now I see them almost every time, I go out shooting and almost every time I return home there is at least one, sometimes two in my road and I have had them living and breeding in my garden as well as under next doors decking and I live in suburban London.

Rats also have apparently doubled in numbers since

Victorian times, and it is said that this is due to all the waste from fast food outlets like McDonald's and KFC not being disposed of properly.

Back in the 1960s, about the only takeaways then, were fish and chip shops and maybe the odd cafe`, and of course, Manze`s Pie and Mash shop in Walthamstow High Street, and on a Sunday, one could go hungry in London if one did not have a cooked dinner indoors as there were no supermarkets then, and due to different laws, most shops were closed by noon. Nowadays, Sundays are busier than Saturdays which was then the traditional market day.

Being the teenage rebel I was, and about sixteen-seventeen years of age, and with Roy now out of the forces. He rented a flat close to Clapton Station.

I would spend days, sometimes weeks, with him and we used to go out shooting in the morning over the reservoirs, which was walking distance, but take our fishing rods with us too.

After the initial first light pigeon shoot, which only lasted an hour or so, we would hide the guns and then fish all day. Once evening came, we produced the guns again and had a second shoot at the pigeon as they returned to roost on the islands and then just as darkness fell, the ducks would return, and we would stand a chance at having maybe one or two of these.

We then traipsed back to the flat, well after dark and I would clean up our spoils and throw whatever we had into a big aluminium pot that was on almost constant simmer on the stove.

I remember one day Roy saying that he did not feel too well, and so he found a doctor to visit. When the doctor found out what he had been eating he gave him a prescription for something like Milk of Magnesia, but rather than it being in a regular-sized medicine bottle, Roy had returned with about half a gallon of this stuff as his system had become completely blocked up at having eaten so much rich food.

Yes, we were eating like Kings, but living like paupers. But they were good times; the best of times, and when we finally moved and emptied that old cooking pot there was enough lead shot in the bottom to fill about three shotgun shells.

The flat we shared was in Knightland Road, Clapton, a two-storey building with a cellar. We had a couple of rooms on the first floor at the back overlooking the garden.

The hallway was dark and cool with a tiled floor and the old Jewish couple that rented it out, lived on the ground floor; there were no other lodgers, and the place was quiet.

I can still remember the smell and the pop sound of when we lit the gas stove with a match, and as I did what cooking there was to be done. I used to light the oven on chilly nights just to keep the place warm.

The old landlady used to potter around downstairs doing whatever it was she did, but she was fastidious about keeping the hall clean and used to wash it frequently, then lay newspaper down to help it dry quicker. I remember once venturing into the cellar and being surprised by seeing all the wet newspapers hanging up on a washing line to dry.

We had no TV or radio so spent little time indoors and were always out and about somewhere.

What time was spent indoors, Roy spent reading and began to find a great fascination in books on taxidermy.

He wasn't one for joining a library though and with books on this chosen subject being quite few and far between and in many cases rare, he used to *borrow them* for the long term, from the reading rooms of many libraries.

Our exit from that flat came about when I think it was Roy, who accidentally set fire to a tea towel, and in a laughing, yet hurried state, threw open the back window and tossed it out, only for it to land on the plastic roof, that was the old couple's lean-to roof!

―――

Flat number two for us, was then in Glyn Road Hackney, a short distance from Hackney Hospital and owned by Mrs Watson and her two yapping white poodles.

Here, we had the ground floor, if not the whole of the house, although I cannot remember the upstairs and I don't remember Mrs Watson being around so I think she must have lived elsewhere?

Anyway, I spent little time here as Roy had now married his first wife, although his lifestyle changed little and he and I, when I was around, were always out together still shooting and fishing.

His keenness for taxidermy remained, in fact, it had begun to grow, and it was while we were here, that we went out one day and shot a pair of Canada geese that he wanted to try his hand at mounting.

By now he had read all about *how,* to stuff and mount birds, and it was now a matter of putting the knowledge he had gained from the books into practice.

With two dead geese in the kitchen, he set about skinning one, then making up a manikin from woodwool and bound it with a fine string representing the size and shape of the body he had removed from the goose.

Being the first bird, he had attempted to stuff, It was painfully slow as from the get-go, he was a perfectionist. An artist right from the start, but in the end, he got there, and it looked better than good for a first try.

It was heavy though and I remember we used 1/8th steel rods to support the thing. The second bird though was now well past its sell-by-date and had to be disposed of.

Late one night I remember we were walking the towpath along the River Lea at about 2 in the morning. Empty barges were moored up and smelled of woodbine, reminiscent of a time when I walked the same ground many years earlier as a very young boy with my dad.

Roy had a 12-bore with him and now, unable to remember as to why we were out so late or as to why we were there? I do, clearly remember him suddenly raising his gun and firing it at something in a tree whose branches overhung the towpath.

The sound of the gun going off at that time in the morning was alarming, as the backs of houses were to our right, the river to our left and my immediate thoughts were, the police will be here pretty sharpish.

After him taking the shot, I saw something drop from the tree and went forward to pick it up.

"Don`t touch it!" Roy called after me, and this alarmed me almost as much as the sound of the gun going off.

I stopped in my tracks and Roy came up passing me, shining a torch at his quarry on the ground. I then saw that he had bagged a tawny owl, talons opening and closing, in reflex, even though it was dead.

"Those talons are needle-sharp and full of dirt and disease, you wouldn't want those to grab you," he said.

This was to be the next on his list of mounted birds and so began his life and career as a taxidermist.

At the age of seventeen and a half, I joined the army and although the first four months were spent in training without any time off to return home. After this, I gained a home posting and managed to return to London most weekends. It was during this time that I looked forward to linking up with Roy and the old crowd. Although he had moved yet again. This time to a big house at 182, Dalston Lane, Hackney where he had a couple of floors and the use of the garden and cellar.

The taxidermist business had taken off big-time for him, and he was being sent all manner of dead creatures to mount and the freezers were packed with fish and small mammals of every description.

Nothing is ever for nothing. No such thing as a free lunch, as they say, and upon my visits, I was often called on to do the messy jobs, like once skinning a mink that had been sent all the way from Scotland.

This stinky mink must have been in and out of the owner's freezer so many times, to be shown off to friends. That by the time it came to preparing it, it was now bloated and stunk to high heaven.

I also had a go at mounting a few things myself under the watchful eye of Roy of course and remember first mounting a tiny shrew and fixing it to a thin plywood base.

Now being married, she, ` G ` helped much with the

artwork in preparing the glass cases, adding foliage and grasses that wherever possible, was taken from the same area that whatever animal of fish had come from.

She was brilliant and very talented at doing this along with the painting of backgrounds and sky. And far more goes into the mounting of dead animals than one first considers.

It was during this time that the two of us took a trip, by bus, to the Welsh Harp reservoir at Neasden, on the North Circular Road. It was wintertime and freezing cold with snow on the ground.

The idea of the foray was in search of a particular bird. A foreign visitor to England. A duck, known as a smew. At the time, only a handful of breeding pairs visited our shores from Russia I think it was, and Roy was mad-keen on bagging the pair.

Arriving early one morning, we spent all day traipsing around that reservoir, ankle-deep in the snow trying to get close enough for Roy to take his shot.

It was late afternoon, shortly before nightfall that he finally bagged the cock-bird as it took off from the water and came within range. A one-shot kill.

During the next few weeks, he returned to the Welsh Harp several times, finally shooting the hen bird too. Although by then, I was back with my regiment and not with him to share his no doubt excitement.

He made a beautiful job of mounting them in a glass case and his first wife, ` G `, with the inner décor.

When Roy died. His then-wife, ` W `, asked if I would like something to remember him by and so I, of course, asked for the treasured pair of cased smew, which now adorns my study.

During the time I had been away in the army, Roy had

met and befriended many people, some good, some not so.

Among the best, was a guy called Lenny Middleton, a milkman that was a keen falconer and fisherman, more of which I shall tell of later.

Amongst the not so good, at least as I thought, was a character called Maurice Hemmant. Also, a taxidermist, that lived in the town of Wickham Bishops in Essex. I could write a whole book on him as even to describe him will make you shudder.

Maurice must have stood over 6 feet tall, was as thin as a rake and had matted unwashed hair, as was the rest of him.

He donned a full black beard, was a chain smoker and stank so that you smelled him before seeing him. His eyes were piercing black, yet for all this unkempt state, he was very well-spoken, well-educated and married to a dumpy little thing with rosy, red cheeks that also spoke very well. The daughter of a Colonel.

The very first time I met this man, he had travelled up to London from the depths of Essex and because he did not like driving in London, he had driven part of the way and then boarded a train for the remainder of the journey.

Just entering the room at Dalston Lane, he reeked of sweat and filth and was wearing what were once corduroy trousers, that were so filthy from where he had wiped his hands on the thighs, that the grooves in the material were clogged and appeared smooth and shiny with in-ground fish slime, blood and God-knows-what else! He was also wearing one black Wellington boot and one green one!

He had made the journey for the sole purpose of

going over Walthamstow Reservoirs with Roy to shoot a coot, a small black duck with white markings on its face and bill and common to most places in and around London.

Staying there at the flat, I got hardly any sleep that night as Maurice would just not stop talking about the forthcoming outing and constantly paced the room smoking one cigarette after another.

"Do you really think we will get a coot in the morning? Do you, Cleve. Do you? Really?" he kept asking me, over and over. And I kept assuring him he would, without a doubt.

It was alright for Roy next door in his bedroom with his long-legged blonde wife wrapped around him, but I endured this maniacal taxidermist and his craving to shoot this duck all night long and by first light had had more than enough of him for one lifetime.

When Roy came in ready to take him over the reservoir, I was only too pleased to remain and let them go and get on with it.

I guess we all see people differently, as people must see us different to the way we think we appear, and in later years, Roy told me that Maurice had been his mentor, just as Roy was mine.

The house at 182, Dalston Lane, was a hive of activity, with people, as well as dead animals, coming and going, constantly.

Also, then, Lenny and Roy had gone into business together, importing falcons from India and in the basement, there were screen perches with Lanner and Saka falcons sitting on top of them.

When Roy had married his first wife, I made myself scarce but threw my lot in with Keith, and our friend Sid, along with two other old school pals who had rented a flat in Markhouse Road Walthamstow, above a disused betting office and slap-bang opposite the now-closed school we all used to go to.

I was not there very much of the time of course, but when I was, the five of us lived like, *The Young Ones* from the old TV series, and life was now a matter of urban survival.

We were well organised though and one of the things we did, was to chat to the girls as they passed by the front door. Discover what schools they went to and on what days their domestic science day was. In so doing, we then conned them out of their cooked cakes and biscuits on that particular day by inviting them in for coffee.

We also had a *bread run*, which meant we would go to the local bakeries and ask for stale bread for fishing, then bringing it back, heated it up in the oven to make it taste fresh again. We also used to scour Walthamstow Market (The High Street) and pick up vegetables and fruit that had fallen from the stalls and I used to provide stuff like tomatoes and runner beans by scrumping the allotments, also occasionally provide meat, in the form of shooting a wood pigeon or two.

It was during this time, that I had also become friendly with the guy Roy had come to know, Len Middleton, and with whom Roy had set up the business concerning falcons.

Lenny was seriously into falconry. He had a Saker falcon,

an Indian bird of prey, and I used to go out and watch him fly his bird to a lure, which is a long length of cord with a small leather sand-filled bag attached to it, a creance. The wings of whatever it was the bird being trained to hunt were tied to it.

It was fantastic to see the bird work and fly and catch this lure in flight and I soon became smitten by the urge to own a bird of my own.

So one day, whilst out with Roy, we caught a kestrel on Walthamstow Marshes, which is far easier than one would imagine, and I ended up training two of these to fly to me. Then, wanting something bigger and more impressive, I then went to Wales with Len, and we caught a common buzzard and what is known as an eyas bird, a bird that has not yet taken its first flight.

The timing was perfect as we watched the two adult buzzards', mob their, as yet flightless youngster. Forcing it to move along the branch of a lone tree in the middle of a field until it could do no more than spread its wings and just glide down onto the grass.

On Lenny`s command of "Go! Go! Go! "I ran towards the young bird of prey and throwing my combat jacket over it, gathered it up in my arms before returning to the small bell tent in which I stayed for ten days, just talking to the new arrival until it got used to my voice; only leaving the tent and, Sheba, as I had now named her, only to go to the loo.

Then, after the ten days, having her manned enough to sit quite peacefully on my gloved left hand, we returned in a van to London.

I was both excited and proud at having this buzzard, that instead of returning to Keith and the boys at the flat, I went directly to my parents' house, just two minutes' walk from the flat to show them my new and unusual pet. It was during this time the police raided the place where they all got busted for smoking pot; and Sheba, upon making an entrance in my mum and dad's house, raised her tail and *sliced* (pooed!) all up the wall!

I kept Sheba, in a small, plastic roofed shed on a screen perch, that was my kid brother's old playhouse, at the end of the garden. I also had a bow perch in the garden for her to sit on.

To *man her*, as one cannot train a bird of prey as one does a dog, I used to walk with her on my hand up and down Walthamstow High Street, and the surrounding area.

I got her used to the various sights and sounds of Walthamstow. Where some people used to ask, "Does it talk?"

This bird had a four-foot wingspan and was over two feet from her head to tail. I fed her on frozen day-old chicks bought from a butcher in Dalston, East London and best, fat-free beef, when I could afford it, as well as mice and sparrows, caught in mouse traps as a source of roughage and weighed her every day.

She was coming on fine and thinking that I had got her used to just about every situation. One morning, the woman that lived in the house whose garden backed onto our garden, shook a blanket from her back bedroom window and Sheba took off.

She flew from Walthamstow to Sawbridgeworth, some twenty-two miles away, almost knocked a woman off her bike and made the local paper, the Harlow Guardian.

The RSPB collected her and put her in, of all things; a parrot cage, the largest thing they had. It was only because an aunt of mine knew that I had lost my bird and had seen the newspaper article, she called my mum, and in turn, my dad took me to collect it. Or so the plan was.

When we got to the place, I was immediately read the riot act about not being able to keep a British bird of prey without a license from the Secretary of State, and was then given the choice of either taking her back home, tending her until fit for release or, for the RSPB to send her to a sanctuary in Cornwall; or so I was told, where she would be released back into the wild once all her feathers had regrown. For putting this beautiful bird of prey into a parrot cage, she had broken and lost her tail feathers, her primary wing feathers and was in a terrible state and did not recognise me whatsoever.

I told the guy that had done this, in no uncertain terms, what I thought of him and his organisation and said seeing as he had already ruined the bird, he might as well do as he thought fit.

To this day, I doubt it made it to the sanctuary and will never forgive them for what they put that poor creature through.

8

BAD MEN AND GOOD SHOOTING

I guess that you must be thinking after a chase by the police with the possibilities of spending the night, or several even, nights in gaol. That I would have or should have, learnt my lesson and just stayed away from Walthamstow Reservoirs.

However, life is too short, and one has to make moments, as they rarely make their own and so on another night at almost the exact same location, reservoir number 5, and now having upgraded again, this time to a single barrel 12-gauge shotgun, I was with my long time close friend Keith.

We found ourselves laying on the side of the banking in complete darkness and just about halfway up the slope in readiness to crawl to the top, to spy on any ducks that might be feeding in the margins when suddenly; we heard a vehicle approaching, moving very slowly along the flat base of the embankment.

There were no lights to be seen and the vehicles` movement was painfully slow. I could not see Keith it was so dark, but I knew he was there to my right and only about six feet away from where I lay.

"Do you hear that?" I whispered.

"Yes," he quietly replied, "can't be water-board though, not at this time of night."

"Not police either," I said, "not without lights."

We remained where we were, silent, still and invisible in the dark of the night. While not far away the vehicle now stopped. The engine was turned off and I thought at first, we were going to be found or even tripped over, we were that close.

We then heard doors open; recognisable as those of a van, then began hearing whispered voices but could not tell what was being said.

This was then followed by metallic sounds coming to our ears; clunking, clinking, sounds like bits of metal hitting against each other. I formed a picture in my head.

These were bad guys! A couple of thieves that had obviously stolen something metallic and were dividing up their swag far away from prying eyes, yet without any idea that we two, Keith and myself, were laying just feet away!

I cannot speak for Keith, but my heart was racing with excitement, as we continued to just lay there and listen to the goings-on not more than twenty or so feet from us.

For what seemed an age this went on, then finally, the van doors closed, the engine started, again, no lights were turned on and the vehicle drove away as slowly as it had arrived.

Once gone, and all was quiet, we moved down the embankment and began feeling around in the grass and darkness where the van had been parked. Brushing the ground with our fingertips, we soon came across a few strange, shaped bits of metal, brass; brass fittings that a plumber might use.

These crooks had obviously turned over and robbed a plumber's merchants or warehouse or something and had had a load of brass away!

It was little things like this that have made my life an adventure, as I knew that others could not have experienced anything the way I did, with the exception that is, of Keith that night. I don't think we did much shooting if any, as we had had our excitement and a talking point to last us a good many weeks.

———

The narrow strip of land that separates reservoirs numbers 5 and 4, was known to me and other shooters as, The Bar. This leads down to The Spinney and a small stand of trees.

One winter's night, in the middle of a blizzard, I had been over the reservoirs shooting with Roy and he, having already downed one duck that had landed close to the water's edge in number 4, I was busy trying to retrieve it by means of scooping at it with a long stick.

The wind was howling, the snow blowing hard and he, Roy, was standing alone on The Bar. I just happened to look across at him and as I did, a pair of teal raced across the heavy snow-laden sky, heard but almost unseen.

It was a moment that I think they call, *a Kodak moment*, and it was as though my mind had taken a still photograph, or more accurately, a short video of the scene, as I saw Roy come up with his gun and first bang one, and then the other, of the two tiny ducks.

A right and left at teal. His gun was vertical as he hit the first bird and beyond the vertical, leaning back, as he downed the second.

It was fantastic shooting and I watched in awe as I saw the tiny birds spin out of the snowy night sky dropping dead into the cold waters, one on either side of The Bar.

On another occasion, we were on the marshes and having had our couple of hours shooting and our breakfast in The Woodman Cafe`. A small group of us were just standing there idly chatting, smoking and laughing before each making our way home when a lone woodpigeon suddenly came speeding across the pale blue sky at a ridiculous height.

All the other marsh shooters just stood looking up, not even attempting to try for the highflier as Roy raised his 3-inch magnum wild-fowling piece with Damascus barrels and fired a single shot into the mid-morning sky.

The bird folded its wings and began to get bigger by the second as it plummeted earthward. It seemed to take an age to reach Terra-firmer, landing just feet from where we were all standing, and I think everyone was silent for a time and in awe at having witnessed such a shot.

When they began talking again, after the jokes and jibes of it being a fluke and dying of shock, things like that. Roy began plucking the bird, only to discover it had been hit and killed by just a single pellet that had struck it in the underside of its beak and gone into its head.

Roy truly was a great shot with both shotgun and rifle and all these years on, I have never even been close to his standard of shotgun shooting, even though I went on to join the army and then on to become Marksman of All Weapons, then finally a sniper when on active service.

Roy's shooting accuracy was not only top class, but his reactions were also fast, and on one occasion maybe a bit too fast.

We were walking across the marsh early one Sunday morning when something jumped up in front of us and he raised his gun and fired before I had even had time to blink.

He then swore and began running forward and I still I had not seen what it was he had hit.

About fifty yards or more in front, he bent down and gently picked up a bird.

It was an owl, a little owl and by more luck than anything else he had only managed to prick it and break its wing.

With more swearing and cursing at himself, he gently picked it up, placing it into his jacket pocket and we took it back to the flat he then had in Dalston Lane. Hackney.

The next day, Monday, he took it to a vet and a pin was placed in its wing. The owl was then known as *Pin Wing* and lived in the airing cupboard where we fed it and tended it for a few weeks before taking it back over the marshes, releasing it back into the wild.

I have had similar things happen to me over the years. Soft moments, if you like. And although I still shoot about once or twice a week, mostly at night, now with night vision equipment when out hunting rabbits, I have had these moments, and know other shooters have had them also.

On two occasions I have had a certain well-known organisation take birds off me, with me thinking that they would tend them and then release them when fit and well back into the wild. Only to find that on both occasions that the birds had been destroyed.

The last one, many years ago now, was a lovely little hobby hawk, similar to a kestrel in looks, that having found injured, I brought home and had it feeding out of my hand and rousing itself, fluffing its feathers with contentment, within just a couple of hours, although its wing did seem to be broken.

I called the organisation in question, and they eventually came and collected it.

The next morning when I called to see how it was fairing, they told me they had destroyed it as it had an infection.

Strange that, as it had seemed perfectly fine the night before other than its wing was drooping and possibly broken. I guess I should have taken it to a private vet as Roy had done all those years previous and then cared for it myself; still, I will know next time if ever there is a next time.

I did pick up a tawny owl one night on the way home from shooting, that had been hit, I am guessing by a car.

I thought at first it was a branch in the road and moved to the opposite side of the carriageway to avoid it.

Passing it slowly, I did however see that it was indeed an owl. So pulled over, got out and threw my fleece over it. I then decided to take it home to check it out and see what damage it had sustained.

I put it into my rucksack and pulled the drawstring so just its head was showing before placing it on the back seat.

On the drive home I then heard a fluttering sound and looking in my rear-view mirror saw that it had climbed out of the fleece and the bag and was now sitting on the rear parcel shelf.

There was not much traffic on the roads at that time of the morning but stopping at traffic lights I had cars both next to me and behind and dread to think what the other drivers must have thought of seeing an owl sitting on my rear parcel shelf.

When I arrived home, I took it to the shed, examined it wearing heavy-duty gardening gloves, as its talons were like needles, and I could feel them gradually penetrating them. There seemed little wrong with it and generally in good health.

Its legs felt fine, its wings also, although its tail seemed a bit bent and off centre. I then placed it in a bucket on the workbench, which I had placed on its side, placed the owl in it and covered the open front of the bucket with an old towel. I then tried feeding it fresh, raw rabbit meat, but it showed no interest, so going to the house, I had a coffee, sorted out the rest of my stuff and soon returned to the shed.

It had now come out of the bucket, looked very alert and as though it was searching for an exit, so I gently picked it up, took it outside and placed it on the shed roof.

It took one look around, then at the near full moon, then silently just flew off across about half a dozen gardens and up into a tall pine tree.

I slept well that night knowing I had done a good deed. Mind you, he had a long flight back to where I had found him unless he found knew hunting ground closer to where I live.

9
PROPER POACHING

During the time I had met Len Middleton, who was extremely skilled and made all his own hoods and jesses for his birds of prey, I also met another guy only known to me as Mac.

He was not into birds of prey or shooting as far as I knew but he owned the van that we had used to drive to Wales. He was a decent enough bloke albeit with an annoying habit of constantly filing his fingernails with the side of a matchbox!

He once took Roy and me out when Roy, without a vehicle of his own at the time, fancied some proper poaching around Ongar in Essex.

It was a Husky van and we had gone out *tooled up*. Roy having a 12-bore shotgun and myself carrying Lenny`s pre-war BSA Airsporter, the type you sometimes see nowadays hanging above fireplaces in old country pubs; the construction of which is about 90% metal with just a short wooden stock.

Lenny`s Airsporter had a Weaver scope welded to it,

and as far as accuracy and power were concerned it was faultless.

We set off this day, driving around the country roads and lanes, Roy sitting in the front passenger seat and I, on the back seat with the air rifle. The fields had not long been harvested of their crops so all that remained was stubble.

Spotting a big cock pheasant some twenty to thirty yards out in the field and feeding on what remained of fallen corn or barley, Mac pulled up by the side of the road and Roy opened the front passenger side window.

"Fancy your luck?" Roy asked me.

I loaded the old Airsporter, leaned over Roy`s left shoulder from the seat in the back of the van and the pheasant ducked down and ran a few yards only to raise its head again a few yards further along the field.

He did this more than a couple of times and I ended up guessing as to where he would show himself again. He came up, right on the crosshairs and `whack!` I fired and saw him waver and go down.

Roy was out of the van like a whippet, running across the stubble, I saw him pick up the bird, quickly stuffing it beneath in his jacket. Then, returning casually to the vehicle, he threw the bird over his shoulder to where I was in the back where I saw that I had killed it stone dead with a perfect neck shot. I was very pleased and was praised by the other two guys for such a good shot.

We then found ourselves near a kind of orchard and it was Roy this time that got out with his 12-gauge. Vanishing into the trees there came a sudden bang! A pause, and then he returned with pheasant number two.

We returned home at the end of the day with three in total and plenty of happy memories as well.

I was never quite sure where Roy met some of these people that he became friends with? But he met two Italian brothers, Carlo and Aldo, and started going all over the place shooting with these guys.

I was not taken so much with either of them so declined offers of going out with them, especially when Carlo took his very young son along all the time.

Carlo had his uses though, as everyone did when with Roy, and he, Carlo happened to be a very good cook, a chef I think by profession.

If he was at Roy's place, there would always be something good to eat and one day when I showed up, Carlo and Roy, had cooked something and insisted I try it. I did and it was lovely.

They then began sniggering after watching me eat and I felt as though somehow, I had been had.

"What's up?" I asked in all innocence.

"Do you know what you have just eaten?" one of them asked, sniggering.

"No, but I am sure you are going to tell me," I said.

"That was an old dog fox we banged off!" one of them answered.

"Then you had better bring me seconds." I said, "this is really good." And it was too!

Since then, I have eaten all manner of birds and animals and become something of a half-decent cook myself and a fox is not that bad, especially when cooked by an Italian chef.

10

FREE FRESH MEAT

I don't know how the other blokes that I met felt about shooting the marshes, and reservoirs. The likes of Ginger, Yogi and Albie, but for me, it was everything, a whole new way of life and one I lived for and thought of all week long, between meet-ups.

I could not wait for the weekend to come around and regardless of the weather, all I wanted to do was be out there on the marshes.

Maybe it was just a hobby for them, just something to do for a few hours before going out on the beer during the night? For me, though it was a passion and when Roy was away in the Marines, I continued to go over Walthamstow Reservoirs, either meeting up with the other marsh shooters, or alone and late at night just for the solitude and to get away from the hum-drum noise that the city gives off.

The night was never a failure or disappointment even if I returned home with nothing, but rather a bonus if I did.

My parents were far from well off, as I have said

already, and I doubt if they had even eaten duck or pigeon prior to me bringing them home but nothing went to waste and I had an uncle that years later, having introduced him to the taste of fresh *wild food,* became so passionate about it, that although he did not hunt or shoot himself, and his wife, my aunt Maureen, refused to cook it for him. He put himself out to buy woodpigeon from Sainsbury`s and started cooking it for himself.

I am not sure if that supermarket now sells woodpigeon. As I did hear that due to it being classed as *vermin,* it was taken off the shelves. Although Harrod`s sell it and charge an absolute fortune for it, as they do rabbit, which in more recent years, is more expensive than venison.

With the coming of celebrity chefs and whole TV channels now dedicated to cooking. Much more in the way of game birds, venison, pigeon and rabbit, are now promoted more than it once was, and with offal; once cheap meat when I was young, and which my mum often bought for my dad. In the way of oxtail for a stew, or pigs trotter or tripe and onions. Now has become an expensive dish and is now in favour with even my grown-up children's friends, who eat it in fancy restaurants and pay top money for it.

To my way of thinking though, rabbit and pigeon is still not mentioned or promoted enough and being that it is classed as *vermin,* simply means that there is an abundance of it. It does not mean it is not safe or good to eat.

On a woodpigeon, for instance, you get about 4 ounces of fresh dark rich red meat, about the same as an average beef burger, but that is where the comparison ends. As one could never compare something as fresh and tasty and good for you as woodpigeon to that of a fat and

`E` number ridden burger, even if it is a well-branded named one.

I can honestly say, I cannot remember the last burger I ate and if I never ate one ever again, I would not miss it. A brace of woodpigeon though, either turned into a stew or with breasts butterflied and just flash-fried in a hot pan with onions would make a really good meal for a man, and a rabbit can easily feed a family.

Butchers' years ago, would have all manner of game. Pheasants, rabbits, hares, pigeons and the like, all hanging up outside their shops but since this country becoming, I do not know what? It`s all a thing of the past now, much in the same way offal shops have disappeared.

I can almost see you cringe at this, but this is the way it was, and it is our loss that things are not like that today.

———

The first rabbit I ever shot I will never forget. It was over the open-air rifle range that ran along one side of the flood field (jungle) and on the opposite side to the allotments that are situated close to Lea Bridge Road, Leyton.

For years I had never seen a single rabbit over there yet often thought that it was prime rabbit country, especially with the allotments being so close with all that tasty veg. However, not having seen any, I never really kept an eye out for them so just concentrated on whacking a couple of pigeons from the trees or off the plots with my air rifle.

And so it was, on a very hot summer's day, I found myself walking the flood field, along the side of the rifle range when just happening to look across the width of the range; I suddenly spied the biggest rabbit you could imagine.

At first, I thought I must be hallucinating it was huge! I felt my pulse start to race and just froze for fear of scaring it away.

Distance-wise it was about fifty yards away with its back to me and close to the brambles and nettles that formed the boundary separating the rifle range, from the Council yard in South Access Road.

I had Ash Mountain and the butts' end of the range to my left, and the deserted firing points to my right. It was about two in the afternoon and the .22 rifle target shooters, that shot there every Sunday morning, starting on the stroke of nine, had long gone, so as ever, I had the whole place to myself.

I crouched down in the brambles and nettles on my side of the rifle range and slowly, very slowly, raised my rifle and took aim. My heart was going like a hammer in my chest, and I was soaked in sweat.

The big rabbit was still there, still munching away and still with its back to me. I did not want to take a shot and risk just wounding it with a body shot, so I patiently waited for it to turn sideways on, in order to take a head shot.

Munching and moving, munching and moving, it gradually turned left, and finally, I now had my chance. Holding my breath, I took a steady aim and squeezed the trigger. Crack! Went the rifle! Shish! went the pellet and I missed with the pellet going high, losing itself in the brambles!

I could not believe it! I was stunned by my own lack of marksmanship as I had plainly fired high and only just missed it.

The rabbit sat bolt upright, startled and looked all around. I remained still, unmoving, almost lost buried in nettles and sharp foliage.

After a long pause it went back to eating again and I, almost moving so slowly as not to look as though I was moving at all, lowered my rifle, re cocked it and placed another pellet in the breach.

For what seemed forever I waited once more for it to get in a position so that I could try for a headshot. I had flies all around me, buzzing and crawling insects but was so intent on the rabbit that nothing else existed at that moment in time.

Finally, there it was again, sideways on, head lowered, eating and not knowing its fate. I raised the rifle for the second time, took aim, squeezed off and thwack! rolled it over.

I continued to look through the scope in almost complete disbelief as the rabbit just lay there unmoving, and then, breaking cover ran through the nettles, the brambles, across the open ground and gained my prize.

How pleased was I and what a size it was too! Holding it by the back legs, as I walked home that day, its ears touched the ground.

After that first rabbit, I saw and shot a good few more over that flood field in the months and years that followed, but never one as big as that first one. And although I have taken hundreds, if not over a thousand since. No other quite held the same excitement as that one, even though now I shoot them with a FAC rated .22 rim-fire rifle and a 17HMR at ridiculously long distances.

The longest to date being, 168 yards at night with a Gen 2+ night vision scope. One-shot one kill.

Years after, my now long-time shooting partner and very good friend Alan, used to come shooting over the allotments and flood field with me, and many a time we have reminisced on just how good the shooting was on that little patch of land, that oasis, in the heart of London's East End.

Just as I was almost ten years junior to Roy, who introduced me to the great outdoors, I am, ten years senior to Alan, and in turn introduced him to the ways of woodcraft. He is an excellent shot both with rifle and shotgun and I would trust no other, on a dark night walking behind me with a loaded gun.

He used to live in Enfield, but many years ago now moved out to the Norfolk/Suffolk borders and has all the shooting one could ever wish for, both pigeon and rabbit and deer and when the season commands, pheasant too.

He is my very good friend and although I do not see him now as much as I used to or would like, when I do visit at weekends, we have some fantastic times together whether we shoot or not.

11

NOT ALL COPPERS ARE BASTARDS

By the time my good friend Alan, came onto the scene and we had partnered up in shooting, I had bought and sold many air rifles and had a BSA Airsporter `S` and he a Titan, which was one of these gas-filled types, rather than the older styled spring powered air rifle.

I was very impressed with the Titan`s accuracy and the way shot after shot could be placed in such a tight group.

I had been having trouble with my rifle anyway and so decided once more to move on and buy another. Always having had a liking for the unusual, quirky, the slightly different, when I saw a company called Brocock, advertising their wares and the quite radical system of charging and loading the cartridges with air, rather than the rifle itself. I just had to get one.

I first bought the Brocock Safari, and how pleased I was when I got it., It was everything I wanted, and just like a real rifle. It was only a single shot bolt action, and the cartridges were about the same size as a 12-bore shell made of alloy.

It was fiddly and time-consuming though in charging and loading each shell with air and then placing a .22 air rifle pellet in the nosecone of each cartridge before reassembling them in readiness to fire, but I loved it and spent hours pumping these shells up and loading them.

The method of charging these shells was carried out using a hand pump called a Slim Jim, which came with it, and much like a Bull-worker exercise machine.

One started off okay, but as the pressure built up so it became harder and harder to pump until after about just eight pumps, my arms felt like they were falling off and I could never charge up shells on the day I intended to go shooting, only the night before, as my biceps would ache, and my arms would feel like jelly.

Then there were the `o` rings and seals that sometimes leaked. So I could spend long minutes pumping up a cartridge only to then hear the air escaping with a hiss and knew I had to do that one all over again. Yes, it was a pain, but still, I liked the system and the recoilless and accurate shooting it gave me.

I persevered with this rifle for quite some time then, Brocock brought out another rifle, the Predator.

It worked on the same system, but this was even more realistic to a real percussion rifle, in that the shells were now much smaller, something like .38 calibre brass and the rifle had a 6-shot magazine bolt action feed.

One had to be careful not to lose the ejected shells though, as, unlike the real thing, these things were about £ 2.50 each and reusable.

After much ridiculing and Mickey taking from Alan, I once more persevered with the loading, pumping and seal changing, but was getting far more accurate shooting than I had from any spring gun, and I did truly enjoy the messing about even with all the aggravation that came with it.

Anyway, ever upward and onward. Getting a little bored with the same old hunting ground, I one day decided to write a blanket letter to about 30 places I thought, *might* be having trouble with rabbits and other pests.

I heard nothing back for three months, but still having the allotments, where I was now known as *pigeon man* ` and having written permission, I felt more secure than when I had been younger and reckless and had shot illegally on the marshes and reservoirs.

I remember the day clearly when the phone finally rang. It was a Monday morning and the guy at the other end of the line asked,

"Do you still shoot and if so, do you shoot rabbits?"

It was a guy called, Alan Day and he had held onto one of my letters going on to say that he had a big problem with rabbits on his golf course.

I could not really take it in for the first few seconds and then when it did, I tried to sound professional.

He was only about a 20-minute drive away and I was there within the hour, walking over some 50 acres of a nine-hole course, spotting rabbit damage, and seeking out their burrows.

I told him, that I would get onto it as soon as possible and then, having taken my leave, I could not wait to tell Alan.

Now, having a legitimate and reasonable piece of land to shoot over, my thoughts then turned to me getting a firearms certificate, as once again, I had seen yet another air rifle and one that could be adjusted to fire at various power levels; from just 2 foot-pounds, for back garden plinking, to a massive 80 foot-pounds for taking out rabbits at long distances. It was the Carreer 707 and the ugliest air rifle I had ever seen!

It looked something of a cross between an over and under shotgun, having one barrel above the other and an underlever cocking handle, like that of a Winchester Western rifle. The metalwork around the trigger area and under bodywork looked to be of tin, with awful gaudy pictures of pheasants and other animals moulded into it. Still, despite its appearance, it sounded the right thing for the job

Finding a monthly air gun magazine with a centre page spread of this rifle depicted in it, I kept it safe as I then applied to the police for my Firearms Certificate.

It took the best part of a year to get my certificate, and I had to buy a gun cabinet and have this fitted securely to a supporting wall before anything else.

On the day that the firearms officer and his civilian helper turned up, I made them welcome, sat down, answered a few questions and then the officer, PC Brennan, asked what rifle I was looking to buy?

Having the magazine to hand, I proudly took it out, opened it at the centrefold showing him my *dream gun*.

I can see his face now as PC Brennan looked at this picture saying,

"What the hell do want a piece of **** like this for?"

I endeavoured to explain, that it had a variable power system, which would suit me for the purpose of shooting both rabbits and back garden plinking, yet before I had gone on, he cut in and started to explain the various powers that .22 rifle ammunition had. Should I want to use ammunition at different power strengths concluding by saying,

"You don't want a piece of junk like that; I'll put you down for a, 22 rimfire rifle."

I could not believe what I was hearing. This copper was putting me forward for a *real rifle*, one that fired *real bullets*! To say that I was overjoyed, would be an understatement and I could not quite believe it! It was like having all my Christmas` come at once.

Of course, back garden plinking was out of the question, but to own and shoot a .22 rimfire rifle, was something I had not even considered unless I had wanted to belong to a rifle club and shoot paper targets. So, if it had not been for PC Pat Brennan, I might still be shooting air rifles to this day.

I also clearly remember the first time ever I went out with my new real rifle. It was the strangest feeling. To walk around in the open, with a loaded rifle and to be completely legal!

Of course, having been in the army, I had done this with a much larger calibre, the L1A1, SLR in 7.62mm calibre, but this was different, and the sense of responsibility was, at first, a bit alarming, for even a tiny .22 calibre bullet can easily kill someone, so every shot has to be thought about far more than messing about with an air rifle.

One must think all the time about the backstop, and just where the bullet will end up if not in the chosen target.

Of course, like so many things, this becomes second nature with practice and the more often one shoots, the easier it becomes.

There has been many a time since though when I

have forgone a shot as not being sure it is safe when using a .22, that otherwise, I would have taken using an air rifle.

Alan, on hearing that I now had my FAC, then soon applied for his.

His dream rifle at the time was also initially, an air rifle. A beast of a thing called a Ripley. It was handmade, costing a fortune. So much in fact, that he could have bought half a dozen rimfire rifles for the cost of a single Ripley, but men must have their dreams and that, at the time, was his.

It was, as I say a beast of a thing, being very heavy with a sound moderator (silencer) that was about the size of a soft drinks can. But it was also a powerful rifle, very powerful until that is, he compared it to my rimfire.

To carry out a comparison check, we set up an old bar stool seat made of almost 2" pine, setting it on its side at about thirty yards distance. We pinned a paper target to it then retired and getting down into the prone position began plinking.

I was using subsonic ammunition which is most suited for a rimfire rifle fitted with a moderator when hunting. The sound is reduced significantly but not so much as seen in the films, for films are no more than just that.

After a few shots, we went forward to check the target and both our groupings were outstanding. It used to be called *keyholing* and now, *clover leafing,* which simply means each shot is passing through the same hole, or as close to the last, making it look like a keyhole or clover-leaf in shape.

However, it was when we looked for bullet penetration and at the back of the pine chair seat; we were amazed, for Alan's Ripley rifle, although the heavy bullet-shaped pellets had gone deep into the wood, my rimfire ammunition had passed clean through it, splintering the back out as though the wood had been of no resistance whatsoever.

The power of this little bullet is quite incredible even out to 100 yards, and beyond. With subsonic ammunition travelling at 1050 fps (feet per second) it is a leveller that's for sure.

Underestimating the power of the little .22 round at first, I never even contemplated long shots, thinking they were unfair and possibly cruel.

One day, however, I was out with Alan, now that we both had .22 rimfire rifles, as he had finally discarded his Ripley, and he too now had a rimfire. When we happened to see three rabbits at the far end of a field. I measured their distance with my rangefinder, as being 112 yards away.

I was not even going to attempt shooting them, but Alan. resting his rifle on a fence post, took aim and using a slight degree of *holdover* (aiming high) went bang, bang, bang and cleanly took out all three.

12

BULLET POINTS AND NEW GROUND

PC Pat Brennan, and his information concerning the various power of different kinds of.22 ammunition had been correct. The lowest powered, although now probably only used at places like fairgrounds, are known as CB caps and of these, I have no idea of the velocity, but they cannot be much as of the short distance they are used over, feet rather than yards. Then there is round-nosed target ammunition known as Eley Zimmer's. Now obsolete since writing this and have been replaced with CCI Quiet

These have a velocity of around 800 fps and basically turn a .22 rimfire rifle into a very powerful air rifle. Which would be suited for say, indoor target shooting at about 25 yards or if carrying out pest control, shooting rats at a short distance.

Using a sound moderator with this ammunition does mimic the sound of a silenced gun one sees in the films as there is no discernible crack or real noise whatsoever from the rifle, only a little more than a phut!

This ammunition must be used on small live quarry,

as it is what is called, *expanding ammunition* and fragments upon entry, therefore being more humane than a solid lead bullet.

Moving up the scale of expanding ammunition. This is the type used by hunters all live quarry. With a sound moderator fitted to the rifle, CCI is the quietest. Although they are only good for say, 30-40 yards on small game.

Next there are standard subsonic, which punch very good, right out to 100 yards and beyond as the bullet travels at 1050 fps.

Moving up in both power and speed, we then come to the standard load for .22 rimfire ammunition; high velocity (HV). This speeds along at what at first seems to be one a hell of a rate, 1250 fps (over 300 yards per second). And even with a sound moderator fitted, it makes a discerning crack! Without a moderator, it can sound very loud especially if hunting at night and is both off-putting to people that hear it being and probably to any wildlife in the area too. I admit I have done and do, at times fire this through my designated day rifle but never at night.

One can also get .22 shot-shells, or used to be able to, which will turn your rifle into a mini shotgun. However, one must remember not to use this with a silencer fitted as it would just fill it with tiny shot pellets and as far as any real use. It has been said one could shoot a mouse in your living room with a .22 shotgun, kill the mouse yet not damage the wainscoting. This I could quite believe and although I have a couple of small boxes of these, I cannot ever see myself finding a real use for them as once when messing about, I shot some tin cans at about five yards distance and not one of the cans was punctured and only barely dented them.

It is said that many years ago when Wild West shows were common (I was lucky enough to have been taken to one as a child) like circuses, these travelled around the country.

The trick shooters that used to shoot balloons in the air and maybe the odd China plate using a six-gun (revolver) used .22 shot-shells, as by using a single bullet would be just a bit too clever. Unless your name happened to be, Annie Oakley of course who, as a teenage girl could shoot a cigarette from her husband's mouth using a .22 rifle at 25 yards with open sights with the rifle rested over her shoulder whilst looking in a mirror; using the refection of the target through the sights.

She supposedly could also shoot a coin from between her husband's fingers. You could see that they got on well.

Generally, the .22 rimfire rifle, which came into being in Victorian times, was meant to be a 50-yard rifle and probably still is, loosely speaking. I say this, as having tested various brands of high velocity and subsonic ammunition they are all good at grouping at 50 yards but then start to open up at 75 yards and beyond.

It is much like finding the right pellet to suit a particular air rifle, so one must find the right brand of a bullet to suit whatever rifle you are using. My own favoured brand that I find above average in my Sako is Winchester subsonic, 42 grain and although I find little difference with any of the various makes at 50 yards, Winchester can take out rabbits up to 150 yards with ease.

Having just about covered the small but deadly, .22 rimfire ammunition, and without going into the .22 magnum ammo. In recent years a favoured calibre of the rabbit hunter has become the .17HMR which stands for Hornady Magnum Round.

This is a high-velocity magnum round, a good bit more expensive than standard .22 ammunition and travels at an astounding 3000fps, or very close to it.

It also fires along a very flat trajectory (with not much of an arc) and so generally what you aim at, you hit. The calibre is tiny though and the bullet head is the same size as the little .177 pellet used in the smallest of air rifles and weighs just 17 grains.

Of course, at this speed of travel, it is a devastating round on live quarry as it is also fitted with a ballistic tip, which basically explodes on contact, causing much damage. It also has a significant drawback; as even if there is the lightest of breezes, or should the bullet happen to hit a small twig or even a blade of grass on its way to the target then it is deflected, and you will miss.

I have given the game away a bit by mentioning the speed of the .17HMR as previously I said that the .22 high velocity was fast at 1250 fps, so, when you then consider the speed of a full-bore rifle bullet it puts everything else in the shade, as my .223 (556mm) travels at an amazing 3,500 fps, that is almost ¾ of a mile a second!

―――

There are many strange, or to my way of thinking, ridiculous laws, pertaining to the world of shooting that I think are worth a mention.

For instance, one can shoot a bird in a tree such as a woodpigeon with a bolt action .22 rim-fire rifle that only fires a single shot before another must be fed manually into the breach. But one is breaking the law if one uses a .22 rim-fire rifle that is semi-automatic.

One can, if in the army and at war, shoot the enemy with a bullet from an SA 80 which fires a .223 or 556mm bullet regardless of the size of the enemy, but cannot legally shoot the smallest of deer in the UK with the same size round.

Primarily the .223 or 22/250 in the world of hunting is classed as a fox rifle although, it would stop a far larger beast even at 300 yards or more.

I think that the people that make these laws have not got a clue about what they are making them about and someone like BASC, British Association for Shooting and Conservation, or the Countryside Alliance should have more of a say in the shooting laws of this country.

There was a total knee jerk reaction after the Hungerford shooting many years ago and then an immediate ban on semi-automatic weapons, except for the .22 rifle, which was then followed by the Dunblane shootings in Scotland, and another reaction by the government of the day, which then banned the ownership of pistols in the UK. This now means that even our Olympic pistol team must travel outside the UK just to practise pistol shooting. And are our streets any safer for all of this? No, not at all. There are apparently more illegally held guns and more killings on the streets of Britain than there was prior to both Hungerford and Dunblane. The law truly is an ass!

Going back to the morning that Alan Day called me, which helped me on my way in being able to shoot using firearms rated .22 rim-fire rifle.

It was just one week later when I got an almost identical call from one James Foulds, asking me the exact same question, telling me that he too had a rabbit problem. Again, I was excited and could not wait to give the good news to my friend Alan.

We now had in total about 300 acres over which to shoot, there were restrictions, but nothing we could not conform to, and so went on to enjoy many months and years of shooting these new grounds.

Then one day, again getting slightly tired of walking the same old ground and knowing it better than the back of my own hand, we, Alan and I, decided to go cold calling on similar sites to which we already had, making sure we spoke to the right person.

By mentioning the places and names of those that had given us permission to shoot; also saying that we could provide references of the places we now shot on. In just one afternoon, we managed to secure another two shoots and also found a butcher that was prepared to take rifle shot rabbits off us.

I just could not believe our luck that day and had now extended our shooting acreage by a further 500 or so.

This was all before Alan, moved out and away from London of course. It was good the way we worked hedgerows and open spaces together or sometimes just lay in wait and picked off rabbits as they showed their heads.

We made good the land that Alan Day had brought us to, making a significant impact on the rabbits there.

Likewise, we did the same on the land that James

Foulds, had called me about and that, along with the other two shoots; by taking them in turn, we had a regular supply of rabbits and managed to keep everyone happy.

At one time we were getting so many rabbits that we were selling them to a dog trainer that fed them to his greyhounds that ran at Walthamstow Greyhound Stadium. The money earned from this was paying for the ammunition we used. Of course, nothing is forever, even though one might like to think so and Walthamstow Stadium sadly closed after sixty years of trading and is as I write this, is now a complex of 500 flats and houses.

Owners and managers also move on, and although I could possibly get back the land that Alan Day, managed and the land that James Foulds had lost, which was also lost to me as a shooting ground. I have since moved on and now have 500 acres of prime shooting ground, abundant with rabbits and other pests that I alone shoot on and control pests.

In updating this edition of my book. Alan has moved back closer to home and now lives with his wife, Debbie on a boat on a river much of the time and I do still see him sometimes, although speak to him on the phone far more often.

He still shoots, occasionally. Mostly keeping magpies and jays off his precious bird feeders, once more, by using an air rifle, for they have their use.

———

Within more recent years, I tried my hand at both beating or what some might call brushing, chasing up the pheasants for the `guns` to shoot, and then a couple of years shooting as a gun on a small pheasant shoot.

Beating is a very enjoyable way for the novice `wannabe` to get involved in shooting. The pay is not great, but it is not about that, it is about being out there, in the countryside and enjoying the company of like-minded people and at the end of the season one gets a chance to shoot on Beaters Day where the guns then beat for you.

Summing it up, shooting in England is far from easy unless you are apt to join a club and pay out a lot of money, but I never have, and hope I never have to, as pest control is a service I provide and there is a mutual agreement between the landowner and shooter. I need the land to be able to follow my sport, and the landowner benefits by me going there and keeping the pests down to a manageable level.

I strongly suggest though, that if any of you do the same, then look after your shoot, visit it regularly and don't desert or neglect it, as there will always be someone else waiting in the wings to jump in and take it from you.

13
PEST CONTROL AND STRANGE NIGHTS

During a time when I was trying to think of other places to shoot other than the flood field and allotments. I came across the idea of contacting pest control companies. Of course, I had no interest whatsoever in bugs or clearing out wasp nests and things of that nature, only shooting and just happened to call a local firm one day and upon talking to the wife of the guy that owned it, was given the chance to shoot some street pigeons or London feral pigeons as they are known, in a warehouse in the heart of London's East End, Brick Lane.

It was the old Truman building where Truman's beer was once brewed and this building had been taken over for the purposes of warehousing and storage.

A new mezzanine floor had been built inside this enormous space and so turned into office space.

Apparently, the workers there had then refused to work in the conditions as these pigeons, entering through broken windows, now roosted on the girder's ledges and pipework high up and basically were messing on everything below, including the workers.

The mezzanine floor had only been in place three weeks and when I went to assess the job it was already over an inch thick in guano (pigeon poo) which crunched underfoot when walked on.

On the day I arrived, I was very business-like, all suited up and looking smart when I met the man that owned the place; explaining to him that myself and my partner, Alan, would return and spend the weekend shooting these pigeons, but it would be his responsibility to dispose of the dead birds once we had bagged them up.

To this, he agreed, and we were back on Saturday, air rifles at the ready, boiler suits and face masks on and lots of ammunition as well as bin bags.

It was fun to start with I must admit, and we shot bird after bird, shot after shot watching them as they dropped fifty or more feet to the mezzanine floor below, or sometimes right down onto the concrete floor, kicking up clouds of dust as they did so.

We could not stay in the building for any great length of time though as one could see the fine dust and filth billowing in the shafts of sunlight coming through the dirty broken windows and it was probably quite dangerous working in such an environment if we had not donned face masks and boiler suits.

By Saturday afternoon, having shot pigeons since early that morning, we were feeling as though this was not fun any longer but just hard dirty work, and by the end of the day, we did not really want to return on Sunday. However, I had given my word, and so on the next day, we returned to carry on the cull.

The shooting was not so continuous now, and we

took far more smoke breaks than the day before, but we carried on and finished by bagging up very many birds and leaving many more on the ledges and girders that were simply impossible to reach.

We were glad to be out of there I can tell you and doing the job as maybe a way into doing other pest control jobs in the future, well, I for one was just happy not to have been called back to do more. It was one of those life learning things that come to all and something that just gets put down to experience.

———

I mentioned earlier about having a designated day rifle, implying that I also have a designated night rifle; I have, and so will explain.

It is another quirky bit of British gun law that says you cannot own two rifles of the same calibre unless they are of different actions. That is to say, one has to be bolt operated, the other semi-automatic, and it is only in .22 calibre that one can own a semi-automatic in this country.

I do though, own two .22 calibre rifles, both of which are bolt action, but one I use for day shooting, the other for night shooting and so, therefore, I am able to own two rifles fitted with the same operating mechanism, but one is fitted with a night vision scope, the other has a day scope on top of it.

This saves all the messing around changing sights over from one rifle to the other as well as constantly re-zeroing them. I have in the past owned semi-automatic .22 rifles, but as they are nowhere near as accurate as a bolt action, have only ever regarded them as fun guns and so sold them.

The scope I use for night shooting is called an image intensifier, which gathers light from all ambient light sources, such as the stars, moon, distant streetlights and light pollution reflected on clouds. This light then gets magnified so that one can see in the dark.

I first used one as a sniper during my time in the army. Which, at the time was fantastic and I was always having the other guys asking me whether they could look through it?

Of course, back then in 1971, these night vision scopes were still in their infancy and cannot be compared to ones nowadays.

For those that have never looked through one. The image one gets is as good as one gets when looking through a conventional daytime telescopic sight, and much like the TV images when war conflicts are filmed at night. The background is coloured green with many features being depicted as black.

I can see rabbits in complete darkness at something close to two to three hundred yards on a night with just a little moon showing, and on a moonless night, I have an infrared laser illuminator fitted to the top of the scope that acts as a torch, (blacklight) invisible to the naked eye and other humans, although able to pick up the eyes of rabbits and other animals.

Of course, one loses the old skills of woodcraft and fieldcraft in having to get close to rabbits with this extended capability of night vision, but this is replaced by more accurate shooting.

Of course, none of this is learnt overnight and it is practice, practice, and more practice that makes one good enough. At night judging distance is particularly difficult; and there are always the off nights when it seems that whatever one does, it just is not good enough and even to this day I still sometimes come home empty-handed.

Even so, I am never depressed at *blanking,* returning home with nothing, as just being out there, seeing things others may never see, is fantastic.

I have watched foxes play; badgers chase one another and scratch at the ground for food. I have seen owls come down on mice in fields and the ghostly barn owl, fly silently just feet from the ground and just yards from where I have been crouching. I have seen bats and deer and hares and fowl on lakes and all this, while others sleep in their beds.

The night-time world is a different world to that of the day, and although dark and sometimes cold and windy, it is rarely frightening, although I have had a few strange and unpleasant or even unnerving moments over the years.

I remember one night before I had a night vision scope, I was out lamping for rabbit and turning the powerful torch on, I would scan the ground from left to right then turn it off and walk 50yards before turning it on again and so cover a good distance in the dark.

I was looking for the reflective eyes of rabbits, so you can imagine, when I turned the lamp on and saw eyes glowing back at me some seven feet up in the air, I was more than just a little startled.

They turned out to be the eyes of a fallow deer standing on her back legs feeding on the top of a tall bush, but it was scary at the time, I don't mind admitting.

On another occasion, this time with night vision. I was out with Alan, on a farm near London Colney.

We had walked the path to where we knew the rabbits would be and I, raising my rifle looked through my night scope to see; of all things, an aeroplane, sitting in the dark in the middle of the field. I guess it was the sheer unexpectedness of it that was startling, and I felt the hairs on the back of my neck rise.

It turned out to be a micro-lite plane and the following day, having called the farmer, discovered that the pilot had made an emergency landing that afternoon as he had fuel pump trouble.

One of, if not, the creepiest experiences I ever had was on a night during the summer.

I had driven along an access road along the side of a golf course I used to shoot over. I had my headlights full on and having stopped at the end of this track, turned my lights, off.

I exited my car, raised my rifle with my night vision scope to look around in an almost 360-degree arc. Then suddenly spied, what looked to be a young man, sitting on a bench in complete darkness just yards from where I was.

I continued to look at him with my night vision, as he looked, as though he was searching for something in a small bag that was on his lap. He seemed to be taking things out of this, holding them up and then returning them.

He did this for what seemed ages and never once did he look in my direction, although he couldn't have failed to see my arrival in the car with my headlights full on.

As I continued to watch him, I also thought, that unless he had some built-in night vision, then there was no way, he could see what he was taking from the bag and putting back in it.

It was positively creepy and so, after several strange and inexplicable minutes, I just got back into my car and drove off.

More recently, I was out, as usual, using my night vision, walking and scanning, walking and scanning, when I suddenly saw two badgers playing, chasing each other around a small clump of bushes some fifty yards away.

Now knowing them to have vicious claws and very sharp teeth, I was not going to disturb them or their antics, so walked away in a 90-degree direction from where they were.

I continued to walk and look and walk and look, bearing in mind, that when my rifle is not raised to my eye, I am as blind as anyone else in the dark.

That is when I heard this grunting, snuffling sound behind me that was approaching a bit too fast for my liking so turning quickly, I snapped on my high-powered torch, only to see Mr Brock making his way straight for me!

I shouted and shooed and yelled, "Get away! Go on! Get!" and the thing just kept on coming for a good few more yards until it came very close before finally getting the message suddenly veering away. I had backed up ten yards or more and just could not believe that a badger would even attempt to see me off! I must have really given him the hump or upset him I guess, but he certainly did the same to me.

14
BIGGER GAME

I have never understood why it is, that deerstalkers are taught to take heart-lung shots yet rabbit hunters', headshots? Perhaps it is because deer stalkers are not such good shots as rabbit shooters, eh? I am being a bit facetious here and was told that it is because if the shot is slightly off when shooting deer, it might result in the hunter hitting the animal in the mouth or jaw, thereby causing the creature to suffer a slow painful death by starvation. However, if this is true of deer, then it certainly must be the same for rabbits? Perhaps it is something more to do with trophies where deer are concerned? Who knows?

Although, again, going against the law in this country, I do admit to shooting deer with a .22 rimfire rifle; albeit the smallest deer to be found in the UK, the Reeves muntjac. All these I have successfully taken out at various ranges with a one-shot kill either with a head or neck shot, and all have dropped like a stone, dead on the spot.

The one exception and this is where I am doubtful of the humane side of shooting a deer in the heart-lung area, was when I came across a muntjac one evening when I was out, foxing with my .223 bolt action rifle.

My rifle was zeroed for 100 yards and the deer, a Reeves muntjac, was about 70 yards distance, standing at an angle facing me. I took a steady aim from a kneeling position, squeezed off the round and hit the deer just behind its left shoulder.

Expecting to see it drop, it did not, yet instead turned and ran. It must have covered 100 yards or more in just seconds, straight into nearby woodland.

Now, these deer are only small, not much bigger than a medium-sized dog, and I now had a hunt on.

Scouring the wood with Alan, we walked up and down in search of the wounded animal as it now began to get dark.

Feeling angry and upset at the fact that the deer should be dead but was not, we then reverted to using torches to find it and all the time I am thinking that this poor thing is in pain and wounded yet should be dead as I had done everything right. We finally found it by the fact that as we got close, it let out the most awful cry. I very quickly dispatched the thing so putting it out of its misery and swore, there and then, that I would never shoot another deer in the heart-lung area.

Once home, upon examining the carcass, my first shot should have killed it, but instead, it had passed right through its body lengthwise at an angle, entering where I had aimed and exiting its right rump area, damaging its lung, liver and much of its intestine too.

It was far from a clean kill, and never would I shoot like that again as ballistics are a law unto themselves and a high-velocity bullet can do strange things to flesh and bone.

I had a friend in the army that was shot with a high-powered rifle of the same calibre too and he was hit in the leg just above the knee. The round then travelled up his thigh and exited just below his groin following muscle grain. I think this says it all, so since then, I have taken out muntjac, which is classed as vermin and a pest in England, by head or neck shots only, and have had some classic shots being more than happy that they were clean kills and the animal felt no pain.

The first deer I shot was an 80-yard neck shot at just after first light on a Saturday morning. I did not even notice it at first, as I was intent on watching a fox just sitting, scratching himself and yawning, probably thinking about finding a place to lay up for the day having been on the prowl all night.

The deer was browsing on some foodstuff in a hedgerow, and it was only when it moved and began backing out of the foliage, I spied it and shot it by shooting over the top of the fox. It fell to the ground as though poll axed, the fox departed at a great rate of knots, and I had suddenly become a deer hunter.

Comparing that first one to others since it was a big beast and I remember just how heavy it felt, as I grabbed it by the legs and swung it up and over and across my shoulders. That was it for the day, one shot, one kill, my first deer and by ten o clock that morning I had it back home, strung up to the tree at the end of my garden and got to work gutting and skinning it. Examining the neck area where I had shot it, I saw that the little .22 bullet had almost passed right through, breaking the neck and chewing through muscle, sinew and cartilage. Death had been instant.

I ate the liver of the beast that morning and it was the

best I had ever tasted incomparable to anything one buys from a butcher or supermarket. I used the whole of the deer except the feet and even these I could have played around with and maybe turned into handles for walking or shooting sticks.

The foreleg meat became a couple of stews, the two back legs, two Sunday roasts and the inner and outer fillets became special meals which I ate with red wine.

I also ate the heart and kidneys. The skin I cleaned and now is hung in my shed, only because I am not allowed it on the wall in the house.

So, nothing went to waste and that is the way I think it should be when hunting animals, one should respect them, even after death and make full use of them as much as possible.

My next deer, many months later, was a twilight shot on a different shooting ground. I had seen it at about 65 yards distant with my naked eye but when looking through my scope (day scope) I lost it in the shadows of overhanging trees.

I swore to myself, lowered the rifle, and then on raising it again, saw a second deer clearly through my scope and with a standing shot dropped it with another neck shot.

This one I cleaned on the spot, leaving the entrails for any prowling fox but again, none of the rest of it went to waste.

Another deer I spotted, again on another one of my many shoots at the time, I could only see as its rear end protruded from some bushes. Kneeling, I watched and waited for an age but instead of backing out into view it moved further in and I thought I had lost it. I think I must have again sworn and standing up, I happened to turn a full 180 degrees only to find that it had gone in a complete half circle and was now behind me and only now about 50 yards away. I raised my rifle, took aim, and dropped it with a headshot.

On checking this one out once I was home. I had expected the bullet to be inside the skull, but having cleaned the head as a trophy due to the tines it had, I found that the bullet had passed right through, entering the skull just behind its right eye and exiting at the back of its rear left jaw which shows you the power of a .22 subsonic. The skull now hangs in my study.

———

I remember well the time Alan shot his first deer. He was still living in Enfield at the time and had gone out by himself after a bunny or two. He then called me quite late, and in a kind of whispered voice said,

"Hi mate, I have just shot my first deer, what do I do now?"

I think I must have laughed out loud but was pleased for him as the feeling of that first deer will stay with me forever, and I knew it would stay with him too.

Having forward notice of what he had done, I rushed around indoors and got a few things together and then set off to meet him. It was dark by the time we met up and I looked around for the deer.

"So, where is it?" I asked.

"It's in that tree," he said pointing.

"What's it doing in a tree?" I asked puzzled.

"I did not want a fox to take it," he replied.

I smiled, but I guess he had a point, as previously when out rabbit shooting, on more than one occasion, we have had cheeky foxes run up and take a dead rabbit before we had a chance to retrieve them.

Leading the way to the tree, I shone my torch up and there, saw the deer hanging draped over one of the lower branches, looking much like Jason's Golden Fleece.

Alan could not stop talking about how he had shot it, where it was, where he was and going into fine detail. He was plainly very excited by it all and I was glad to see it.

Getting the thing out of the tree and now by torchlight, before setting about gutting it and removing the inedible bits, I took some photos of him with his trophy. I then bloodied him by marking his face with the creatures' blood, and then producing my hip flask, I toasted him as we had a snifter of bourbon.

He was made up by all this pomp and ceremony and I did it only to make the occasion as special and as memorable as possible.

I then set about taking out the good stuff; the liver, heart and kidneys placing these in a clean plastic bag.

Like me, Alan also ate the things he killed and was really looking forward to having a fry up the following morning and then, after a week or so of hanging the creature, getting stuck into the venison meat.

Having sorted it all out we went back to his house and strung up the carcass in his garage. His wife, Debbie went on as many a woman would do, saying that she wanted nothing to do with the cooking of it, but in the end, came round and when it looked like meat and not the dead thing it was, she cooked it although may not have eaten it.

It was the talking point of all his friends that turned up during the time it remained hanging in the garage and

Alan, like me, thought that the liver and in fact all of it was far better than any shop-bought meat.

Since then, now that he lives in the countryside, Alan has shot far more deer than I and is very proficient at gutting them, butchering them and making them ready for the table.

15
FOOD FOR THOUGHT

Thinking of Debbie and her not wishing to prepare `game` like deer, rabbit, pheasant, pigeon and things of that nature, along with my own wife May, having the same dislike, started me thinking of just how we have become so far removed from accepting, if not actually knowing, where the meat we eat comes from and how generally we now view meat.

I have heard that many young and even not so young children are not even aware of where milk comes from and do not think beyond the plastic bottle it comes in. Similarly, with meat, they see it all bright red and nicely wrapped in plastic wrap on a polystyrene tray in a supermarket yet have no concept that what they are taking home to eat was once a living, breathing animal.

I think this removal or disengagement is far from good and kids should be aware that beef burgers come from cows and sausages from pigs. And why on earth vegetarian food mimics real meat, is quite beyond me?

Food waste in this country is also a cause for concern.

Foodstuffs are being thrown away. It is said that about a third of all we buy in supermarkets and shops goes straight into the bin. Of course, all this waste may not be meat, but I am guessing much of it is and I am also guessing that whereas my mum and her mum before her, used to use leftovers from one meal to make something for the next day or even the day after that, this is now not the case.

This is a tragedy, and besides being a total waste of money, it is also disrespectful of the animal and also a cause for the food industry to produce more and so go headlong into intensive rearing and farming.

With fridges and freezers, there is no excuse for cooked leftovers to be thrown away and something; say a rabbit stew for instance that is cooked on a Monday, should there be any remaining, can easily be frozen when cooled and then later, turned into a pie by the simple matter of putting a crust on the top and there you have it, another meal.

With the fast pace at which we all seem to be living nowadays and all of us chasing our tails, one would have thought this method of cooking and saving would be something to be embraced. It only takes about the same amount of time to re-heat an already cooked stew or pie, as it would, stick a ready-meal full of `E` numbers and preservatives into the microwave.

With a country fast becoming more and more obese, following in the footsteps of America, from a point of just good health, we should be eating more meat such as rabbit and venison and even grey squirrel maybe? They are another pest in the British countryside and a threat to our native red and having eaten squirrel on more than one occasion, I can, in all honesty, say, that it is good and tasty and what is more, like all wild animals and birds, fat-free.

These wild creatures are the athletes of the world and those not raised in pens, sheds, or left just standing in fields or any other captive space, so, therefore, moving around as they do, the fat is burned off and one is left with pure muscle and good to eat meat.

Here's a thought, road kills. Driving through the countryside we pass so many pheasants and even deer that have been hit and killed by our cars. Yet, how many of us just pass it by, but a pheasant can make a fantastic Sunday lunch and one would be charged much for it if served up in a top restaurant. Similarly, muntjac deer could provide a family of four or even six with several top-quality meals and to me, it tastes much like lamb.

Now I not suggesting that you should just pick up any old roadkill, but if one drives the same route most days and does not see a dead deer by the roadside, one day, but the next day does, then it stands to reason it has not been there that long and therefore pretty much safe to eat. In fact, muntjac is the safest of all venison to eat, as living on a diet of much stuff that other deer species do not, it is free from parasites within the meat and a quick look at the dead creature's liver will soon tell you that it is good to eat and as long as it is not milky looking, streaked, or spotted and looks the way liver is supposed to, then yes, cook it and eat it and you will be eating the best meat you have ever tasted.

I remember one weekend very many years ago when young. Keith and I wanted to get out of London so hopped on a train to Cheshunt in Herts. We had fourteen shillings and sixpence in old money between us, a couple of fishing rods a shop-bought Vesta Beef Curry one large potato, and a dog, Roy`s adopted corgi.

We found a quiet out of the way place on the river, and began fishing, having stopped off and spent some of the money on dog food and a pint of maggots. We caught nothing other than tiny little bleak which I did not even bother trying to gut and clean but just threaded onto some wire and cooked them over an open fire. Keith ate the curry and the potato, and it ended up with him being the one that was sick.

I am again, not saying that you should all go out and start catching and eating freshwater fish, I am simply telling you of what I did and that it did me no harm.

I have since also eaten pike, bream and perch and eel all fresh caught. Bream was the only disappointing one where taste is concerned, as it tasted watery even though the meat was chunky looking much like cod.

Pike is good if it comes from the correct river or lake and from one that has a gravel bottom rather than a muddy one. Perch is great and over an open fire is crunchy and crisp although it has plenty of small bones. Eel is very good; it is meaty, solid and if boiled, makes its own jelly if left to cool. To buy even a small tub of jellied eels from a supermarket is very expensive nowadays but they are out there, in the rivers and lakes of Britain and many anglers that catch them by accident tend to throw them back, why I will never know?

I am guessing that had they gone to the bother of cleaning and cooking them, they would not be throwing away perfectly good and healthy food.

16

NOT SO MUCH A TREASURE MAP AND A NIGHT ON A BOAT

Another adventure Keith and I once had was when I came across an old map and I mean an old map; this thing had canvas backing, was brown and cracked with age so could have easily been dated from fifty years before our time, putting it close to the turn of the beginning of the 20th century. It was interesting though, with few roads marked on it but had some great place names. We decided we would pick one of these strange-sounding places, pack up some stuff and just head off for a few days. The place we chose was, Southminster in Essex and the Denge Marshes.

It looked to be everything we wanted for a weekend's shooting; remote marshland, probably teeming with birds, so we packed our stuff, a small tent, some food, sleeping bags, guns (12 bores) and enough ammunition to start WW3.

Neither of us drove then so we took the train and chatted enthusiastically all the way, about what might lay ahead and what adventures we would have.

As the train pulled into the station, we had a really good feeling about this place and even though the film had not yet been made, upon seeing it, many years later. Southminster was much like something out of the Railway Children.

With thoughts of walking the marshland and salting's and banging away at duck and pigeon, we exited the station, only to find, fields and farmland and anything but marshes. Because of this ancient map, the marshes must have been drained many years previous.

We must have walked miles that day, hardly seeing a house or person. We were hot, fed up and our feet were now sore, and our backs were aching with all the stuff we had bought with us. We knew we could not just set the tent up in a field and besides, we had not even seen a bird in the clear blue summer sky.

The first and only, farmhouse we came to, we decided to knock at the door and ask for some water and upon doing so, I began to explain to the very nice Mrs Fisher, exactly what we had done and asked if she might know of somewhere we could pitch our tent for the night? She was kind enough to let us onto one of her fields and we thanked her kindly.

The fields had only recently been harvested and rectangular bales of hay were strewn all over. I think it was probably me that had the idea of gathering some of these up and building a kind of wall around our little tent so that we did not stick out like a sore thumb in the middle of nowhere.

This we did, and now having a nice little camp we prepared for a good night's sleep with plans of returning to London the following day.

It must have been about two in the morning when

Keith woke me to the sound of a kind of strange, faint scratching.

It was absolutely pitch black in that tent just as it was outside, as there were no streetlights or even ambient light as there was nothing there, only dark fields.

We switched on a torch to look for the mysterious scratching and there, in the tent on the thick plastic groundsheet were beetles, lots of them, big black and crawling. Some had managed to roll on their backs and were frantically trying to right themselves, but they were big, and we were there, in a tiny tent and were stuck with them.

I am guessing they had come out of the bales of hay or straw or whatever it was we had surrounded ourselves with, and even though harmless, seeing them and being with them on the plastic groundsheet made our skin crawl almost as much as they were crawling.

We got them out of the tent, but I don't think either of us got much sleep that night and in the morning, we were gone, back to the station.

Waiting for the train and the return journey to London we noticed on the platform square tins piled up, the kind I remember seeing in off licences that held either Arrowroot biscuits or Smiths Crisps. Anyway, being curious, we went up to these and again heard a sound coming from them, this time a kind of soft rustling. This turned out to be maggots!

Yes, the only thing Southminster seemed to be famous for was a maggot farm! A place full of nothing but creepy, crawly things.

We never fired a single shot that weekend but certainly learned a lesson. Never go to Southminster again and never rely on old and out of date maps.

Thinking of that tale reminds me of a time when my dad used to pick a place on the map and take us out in the `combination`, motorbike and sidecar when we were just young kids.

One Sunday, with my mum on the back and me and my brother, Jeff and our sister Janie in the sidecar, we set off to a place called Shell Haven in Essex. It was a desolate place and dark rain clouds were gathering. There was a single windblown twisted tree by the side of this empty B-road when the rain started, with both our parents getting soaked as we three siblings sat bored in the sidecar.

The view we had was like something from a Sci-Fi film and in fact, it was, for the only features on this flat barren landscape were huge silver domes reflecting the black clouds and the lightning as the storm finally broke.

I found out, many years later that it was this place, Shell Haven, which was used in the film, The Quatermass Experiment but, is an oil refinery owned by Shell Oil; so, that's now two places on my list of never to go to again.

Years later, my wife May, having American relatives, invited her cousin Kevin over to London as she heard he was going on one of these around the world road trips having come out of the army where he had served in Vietnam. I had been in the British army at the same time and having written letters to one another, Kevin and I had become pen pals long before meeting up, so when we did finally get together, we hit it off at once and were already the best of pals.

Kevin was a great loveable guy, a cool fun-loving Californian, always smiling and chilled out, looking much like the singer, Kenny Rogers, with his black-blond beard and shoulder-length wavy hair.

Of course, when one drinks, one gets all the best ideas, and at about two in the morning we had, well I did, came up with the idea to go fishing.

Of course, we had no bait, no transport and even if we had we were too drunk to drive. We had no real suitable clothes either, and it was raining, but still, we went and walked from Walthamstow to Tottenham Hale and along the River Lea before we started to sober up and then feel the cold through the wet. All Kevin kept saying was,

"God damn, God damn man!" So finally, looking for a place to hold up we climbed into one of the small craft that was moored along the riverbank. Crawling in, we soon fell asleep, each of us on a vinyl padded bench, one on each side of the small interior of this two-berth boat.

When we awoke at the first grey light of day, with mist on the river and shivering from the cold, the first thing I noticed was that my nose was about an inch from the ceiling of this boat. The second thing I noticed was the spiders, hundreds of them, right in front of my eyes and all over the inside of this craft!

Lesson: Drinking and shooting never go together, the same can be said for fishing.

Alas, Kevin died at the very young age of just fifty in the Veterans Hospital in Oregon. It was said, or at least hinted at, that it was due to a dose of Agent Orange, a spray that was used in Vietnam to kill off the foliage during the Vietnam War where he had spent two years as a Marine.

17
A NARROW ESCAPE AND GRAVE SECRETS

During my youth and teenage days living at Camden Road, Walthamstow, I just happened to be standing outside one day when I saw a girl walking along on the other side of the road with two beautiful short-haired black Labrador dogs. Never being backwards in coming forward, I went over to her and started chatting as young blokes do, in the hope of both pulling her, and maybe taking her out and using the dogs when out shooting.

I don't mind admitting that both were very fit looking, and I am not just talking about the dogs. Her name was Pamela, and the dogs were mother and daughter, Juno and Kate and very obedient.

Well, I did date her, and we went out to the cinema and things like that, then one summers evening I took her and the two Labs over the flood field, which was then, as I say, like a miniature jungle.

I thought it would be good to get the dogs used to the sound of a 12 bore shotgun at close quarters and being the rotten shot I was, never did hold out much hope in bagging any pigeon but it was a warm summers evening and a Saturday, and we settled in this clearing as I waited for a pigeon to wing its way home to roost on one of the reservoir islands the far side of the marshes.

After a while, one eventually came over, I raised the gun and fired and missed, shortly after another came over, then another and I had fired three rounds and as expected, had three misses, but the dogs had behaved themselves and were not in the least bit frightened of the gun going off.

With the gun reloaded and me, kneeling in front of a bush, a man wearing a light grey suit suddenly stepped out in front of me, grabbed the barrel of my shotgun and pulling it out of my hands said,

"I'll take that son!"

At the very same moment, another guy appeared behind me, also wearing a suit saying that they were policemen and that I was under arrest.

Thinking back, there were so many things wrong, and so many things that could have gone wrong, but being young and taken, as I had been, by total shock and surprise, I did as I was told and handed over the loaded 12-gauge shotgun. As they said that they were going to take me to the local nick, which was Leyton.

I then said to Pam, who by now was in tears. To make her way home to my place and tell my mum what had happened.

In the meantime, these two coppers, obviously without a clue as to where they really were, then asked me to show them the way out to South Access Road, as that was where their car was parked alongside James` Park.

After getting over the initial shock of what had

happened, my brain began working a bit clearer now that I had calmed down.

Also, the fact that one of these idiots was not lying dead in the field at my fee was a relief, having grabbed hold of my loaded shotgun by the barrel, pulling it towards him, not knowing whether my finger had been on the trigger or if the safety might not have been on.

I now had some fun with these two dolts in their light-coloured suits and led them a merry old dance through thickets, brambles and nettles until we finally reached the road and their car; which I might add, was not your everyday police car either; and was, in fact, a Hillman Imp and even that was coloured grey.

I think I was more nervous then, as I was expecting a marked police car, but taking them at their word and them having my gun, cartridge belt and even the three empty shells I had fired, we climbed into the vehicle and drove off to Leyton Police Station.

Once there, having given my name and address I then waited for what seemed to be forever in a room until finally, my dad arrived. Things were then said, and, in the end, I was told to report back on the Wednesday evening to be officially charged.

Now, although I had been shooting on and going over this piece of land for a good few years and not ever having thought of it as actually belonging to anyone. I was now facing no less than fourteen charges, ranging from breaking and entering, as at one time a fence surrounded this land. From trespassing with a loaded firearm to shooting in the vicinity of children.

There was even talk of getting the Transport Police involved because the cartridge belt which I had made by hand, had a piece of leather incorporated in it with the initials B.R.M.M. stamped into it. This leather was apparently originally a window strap that was used to pull up and secure the window on a steam train, which I had found somewhere along with a leather horse` girth strap that I had used as the belts` buckle.

Also as previously mentioned, because of the danger of the possibility of me falling down one of these hidden wells that were scattered throughout this jungle, I used to carry gas fitters smoke pellets in case I ever got into trouble and needed to attract someone's attention. These, the police told me, were going to be sent away for forensic testing.

I don't mind admitting, from that Saturday to the Wednesday, when I was told I had to return to the cop-shop to be officially charged, I did not get much sleep for worrying.

Finally, at the designated time, now suited and booted and looking as though I was about to go out dancing for the night or for a job interview, I made my appearance at Leyton Police Station again with my dad.

Now, this is where it all gets quirky. I remember I was sitting on a hard wooden bench inside the police station, while my old man went up to the desk and started speaking to the Sergeant.

He could not have said much as he was there no time at all and I was out of earshot as to what was being said, but after just a short time, the Sergeant went away soon to return with all my belongings, including even, the three empty shotgun shells, only minus the smoke pellets. These were all then pushed over the countertop to my dad who signed for them, and we left, without another word ever being said.

Now my old man was not the sort of man to cross, so I

never did ask him, ever, as to the whys and wherefores of that night. I did know though that my bacon had somehow been saved and for that, I was more than grateful.

It did cross my mind though, over the years, that perhaps these two coppers were maybe not on their own patch, so maybe had no jurisdiction being there? And just what were they doing dressed in whistles (suits) wearing collars and ties tramping around a place like a flood field? And why a civilian car?

It was all too weird for me, but miraculously I had somehow got away with it and so was never charged or ended up in front of the magistrate or stuck with a criminal record. It had been a close call though, very close, but somehow, I had managed to escape the clutches of the law.

I heard many things about my old dad after he died from his eldest sister, my aunt Betty, but even she would never elaborate on things and seemed to feel awkward at answering questions about him.

He was an army man, 16th 5th Lancers. Lying about his age and joining up two years before he could have as he had a love of horses. Being first sent to India he had then volunteered for 6 Commando and was duly sent back to England, where he was trained to blow up bridges, before being sent to France as he was an excellent swimmer.

My aunt then said, as my dad never ever spoke of the war or his time in the service. At home to us. That he used to come home in civilian clothes, never in uniform, and that he had said to her once, that he was working undercover in Scarborough, living in a property paid for by the military, monitoring the comings and goings in the docks there.

Now whether any of this is true, and whether he was some sort of James Bond figure I cannot say, although I would like to think so. My aunt is now long dead.

I will say though that after his death on Boxing Day 1986 at the age of just 66, going through his belongings, I did find a letter of commendation and thanks signed by the Mayor of Wanstead, but it failed to say what it was for?

I also made some enquiries through military records, and it could well have been that after his time in India and then France, he could have worked in Scarborough for what is now known as GCHQ. I guess we all have our secrets and some we take to the grave.

18

NORFOLK GUNS AND GAME PIE

Having started shooting a rifle at the tender young age of eight, even though it was not much more than a glorified pop gun, I was always something of a natural with a rifle, although shotguns were a different kettle of fish and even though I have improved much over the years, because of lack of practice, I have never felt it as natural to shoot a bird in flight, or a rabbit running using both lead and follow through as one does with a shotgun.

I know I should get more time in on shooting clays, but I also have not really got the passion to shoot shotgun as I have a rifle and so this makes for an easy cop-out, I guess.

Likewise, although I have fired pistols, even classifying Marksman with the Browning 9mm in the army, then more recently firing the Glock 17 in France; my enjoyment still comes back to the rifle.

During my working life, working as I did in Close Protection for two decades, I have met and rubbed shoulders with a good many celebrities and stars of both TV and film and through this was invited on a pheasant shoot a few years ago in Norfolk.

The guy that invited me was down to earth and very friendly, but I remember thinking as the date got nearer, that, for one thing, I had nothing to wear other than full camouflage clothing, and I knew none of the other guys that were going to be shooting, I was getting nervous.

I did not even have a shotgun of my own. So, when the day came, besides being the last to arrive, as some idiot youngster at a garage had given me wrong directions; I very much felt like the new kid on the block and totally out of my depth.

When I did finally arrive at the venue, I was made to feel very welcome though, then having been driven out to meet the rest of the men who by now were already in the field, I soon started to feel a bit more at ease.

The weather was atrocious that day, as it had snowed hard the night before, another reason for my lateness in arriving. There must have been about a foot of snow on the fields. My only known contact there for the day was Colin, and it was he, that was the big chief and organiser. He was also the guy that kindly loaned me a nice little French side by side that fitted me well and put me at my ease from the start.

In freezing cold conditions and shin-deep in snow, the guys picked their peg numbers, but me, being the invited outsider, was designated a place at the end of the line for the first shoot.

I guess this was in case I did not perform correctly, or maybe they were a bit wary of a stranger in their midst with a gun? Anyhow there I now stood waiting for the beaters to do their thing. Then the birds started coming over and with sudden shouts of "English!" and the other guys, with guns raised to the sky, but not shooting; it took me a short while to cotton on that these birds were English partridge, not French, so I now felt even more apprehensive in case I shot something I was not supposed to. I was not having fun.

Then as a recognised bird, a big fat cock pheasant came towards me from the left, I came up on it and bang, nailed it with the first barrel!

With the bird's speed and momentum, it curled into a ball bowled past my position and another two pegs and when it hit the ground, continued to roll, before stopping dead just in front of the line. The guy to my right turned to me and said,

"I would not even have tried for a shot like that. You wiped my eye you did; you wiped my eye."

I did not know at the time whether this was a good thing or not, but then after that first initial drive, gathering on the truck to go off to the next one this guy was singing my praises all the way.

Thing was, I had now set myself a kind of benchmark for the rest of the day, so even this did little to make me feel much better.

It all worked out okay in the end though. The men from Norfolk were a good crowd, the day ended up well with a big mixed bag of pheasant, partridge, pigeon and a hare and it was one of the known guys that ended up shooting an English partridge and they laughed about it but did not let him forget it all day long.

We, then having been allowed a pick of the birds, got changed into suitable dry clothing and met up at a pub where a three-course meal had been laid on and the talking and drinking would have gone on late into the night. I brought back two brace of pheasant and the same of woodpigeon, as no one else seemed to want the pigeon. I also had shot about four or five pheasants myself by the end of the day.

With a long drive home in front of me, I had rationed myself to just one glass of red wine with the meal, then going around and thanking everyone, I said my goodbyes and headed off back to London.

Having written many times for various shooting magazines over the years, including one for Shooting Times, I promised Colin I would send something in about the day and see what happens. I did, and it was printed, so I sent a copy to him which might have gained me the invite for the following year.

This time it was rain, not snow and horizontal rain at that. Unlike the first year, this time I was the first to arrive, and as I sat in my car in the car park, I could feel it rocking and being buffeted by the force of the wind against the side of it. So much, that I did not even want to get out of my car, the weather was so bad, but soon the others started to arrive so there was no turning back.

The day itself was much like the previous year and to get an insight of just how the other half lived was good, as there was a lot of camaraderie between the men, the beaters worked their socks off, the bag of birds was good and beat the previous year by several beaks and I had managed to book a room in a local hotel so therefore stayed on and had a few beers and yes, I enjoyed the difference of what I was generally used to. Whether I would do it and shoot that way often is another matter, for one thing, I just could not afford it.

The one-shot one kills with a rifle at distance is more favourable to me. I have had short distance kills too of course, but I have also left short shots thinking them not sportsmanlike.

Of course, if I were shooting to put food on the table it would be different, as one would not hesitate whether the shot was sporting or not but more of a necessity.

I am also not of the kind of person that thinks a good day's pigeon shooting is over 100 birds. As for one thing the game dealer will hardly give you the money for them that you have spent on the shells and unless you are going to give them to all your friends, neighbours and their friends too, what are you going to do with 100 or more woodpigeon? Far better I think to bag just a few brace, then clean them, freeze them and eat them.

I tend to do this, then at Christmas sort out the freezer and have a large selection of not so usual meats on the table for friends to try.

I remember many years ago now, that my friend Keith came around with his wife Lynn, and I had laid on this quite splendid spread, a smorgasbord in fact, including game pie.

It was clearly marked as such, and Lynn, having already had a reasonably sized wedge, commented on how nice it was then going on asked what was in it?

I said that if she liked it, which she obviously did, then she should not really ask, but she insisted and so I told her.

"Well, it has rabbit, pigeon, squirrel........"

"Squirrel!" She shrieked out and Keith on hearing this said,

"Yes, squirrel," and then made an ear scratching, face

cleaning motion with both his hands held the way a squirrel does, paw-like to his chin.

Well, Lynn then went into one, put the rest of her pie down on the plate, despite her saying just seconds before just how good she had thought it.

I suppose with her husband mimicking a squirrel and her forming a mental picture of the animal it was all a bit too much for her.

Strange though, as when eating a beef burger, one never thinks of a big, brown-eyed cow standing in a field, or if having a KFC how many of us think of chickens, or a baby lamb skipping around in a field when we are tucking into a Sunday roast. What strange and complex creatures we are.

19
KEYSTONE COPS AND SHOOTING STARS

I have only tried netting rabbits twice in my life and both times were very memorable. I was working as a bus driver the first time and the route I had was town and country, well, semi country anyway, as it was from Walthamstow, northeast London out to Loughton in Essex.

I had seen rabbit movement even during the day at the side of the road as it led down into Loughton Town and could see that the ground was sandy and therefore easy for the creatures to burrow into. I mentioned this to a work colleague of mine, Sean, and he had said that he had noticed the same and then suggested we net them one day to which I agreed. Sometime later, when we both had a day off during the week, he turned up with a ferret in a sack and a bundle of purse nets.

I told him that I had never used ferrets before; not even handled them and I must admit knowing their reputation for being vicious little critters, I was not too keen to handle this one. Sean said not to worry as this one was his brothers, and he was used to it.

We set off in Sean's small van and parking close to where we had seen the rabbit movement, walked into the edge of the forest and he began showing me what to do as regards setting the nets. It's not hard but a little time consuming as one has to find the warren and hopefully all the holes leading in and out of it and with some being hidden in nettles and brambles they are not always easy to see and sometimes harder to get at but in the end, we thought we had them covered and then Sean, taking the ferret from the sack, introduced it beneath one of the nets and into the hole and into the maze of burrows. Then it was just a matter of watching and waiting. We did and nothing happened. We waited some more, and still, nothing happened. Finally, the ferret appeared as if to say, `Why am I here? ` and so after a long time we decided to pack it up as the rabbits must have all been on holiday or something, for they sure as anything were not in their little holes.

Being now early afternoon Sean said that he knew of another place a bit further out in Essex that might be worth a try. I was already bored but agreed to go and take a look if that's what he wanted and so, with the ferret safely back in the sack and the nets gathered, we set off for venue number two.

Twenty minutes later found ourselves driving slowly down a country road with Sean looking out of his window saying,

"I am sure this is the place?" but I sensed some uncertainty in his voice, although never said anything, and again, having parked up we gathered the moving sack containing the ferret and the nets and began to set off across these very large fields, the first one being skirted on one side by a well-kept hedge; obviously being the division of someone's garden and the field that ran next to it.

Sean is a great guy and we have kept in touch over the years. He is always cheerful no matter what. Anyhow, we tramped over a couple of big fields, obviously part of a big working cereal farm, until at last, we came to a kind of hedge with a couple of lame and miserable looking trees set into it. Just a token of what probably once was a nice well-kept hedge full of birds and insects and all the other things one should find in such a place. Yes, I like hedgerows and think they should remain a fundamental part of the English countryside. Ireland still has them, and they get by, so why not England?

Seeing some sign of rabbit and a few holes in this pathetic hump on the landscape, we got to work for the second time that day setting the purse nets and introducing the ferret from the sack into one of the holes. We then waited and waited and waited some more and yet again, nothing! Perhaps the last lot of rabbits had phoned this lot to tell them we were on our way to see them, as this also was a barren warren and so we decided to pack it up and just put it down to experience, or rather a lack of.

With Sean carrying the wriggling sack, we set off back towards the van talking and laughing and I happened to look up and saw a policeman suddenly step out of the well-kept hedge we had passed and then step back in again. This copper had not even been subtle about it, for I had spotted him from 200 yards or more and it looked like something from a comedy routine.

I told Sean what I had seen, yet we kept walking in the direction of the van as we did not really have anything to hide and besides, we were in the middle of an enormous field so it was not as though we could go anywhere else.

At last, we came to the hedge and knowing what the policeman was going to do, it was by no means of a surprise when he stepped out just in front of us. In fact, it was quite comical, although neither of us laughed out loud as that would have been asking for trouble.

With the expected words,

"Okay lads, now what have you been up to and what have you got in that sack?"

We endeavoured to explain that we had been netting for rabbits but not having had any luck had decided to call it a day. The copper then asked if we had a car and where it was, knowing all the time that we did have transport as his colleague was already there, standing by it waiting for us to join him.

Having then arrived at the roadside, each of us was taken to opposite sides of it and I was asked to sit on the kerb.

Sean with policeman number one and me with number two, we were then interrogated for a time and asked who owned the van, what was in it, what was in the sack, blah, blah, blah?

I thought it quite amusing at first as these two `not so bright in country matters` coppers asked us if we had been hunting for badgers? Now, as I say, I had never been ferreting before that day, but even I knew that rogues that kill badgers have terriers with them and shovels for digging. We had a sack with a fed-up ferret in it, wanting his dinner.

It then started to get worse when copper number one asked copper number two to get on the radio to check out the index number of Sean's van as he, the first policeman started to rummage around in the back of it.

There was not much in the back of the van, some old blankets or rags, I think. But then this copper, using his finger and thumb picked up this furry thing, this object, and slowly removing it, asked Sean what it was?

Even I could see what it was from where I was still sat on the other side of the road and could hardly contain myself. As it was, of all things, a fox stole! Complete with purple satin liner and flattened head with glass eyes! This turned out to be something Sean`s young daughter played with when dressing up but the policeman had obviously never seen one before and just stood there holding it at arm's length as though it might bite him!

To really make matters interesting, policeman number two then came back by saying that the index mark (registration of the van) belonged to a red Cortina or something and not the white van that Sean had and started asking more questions of him.

Sean, swearing that the van was legitimate, legal and everything else, after some lengthy time, copper number two checked the number again only to discover that he had got it wrong and yes, everything was correct.

With no rabbits and having come across probably the two dumbest policemen in Essex it certainly was a day worth remembering.

The last time I went ferreting for rabbits was on the farm that both Alan and I had permission to shoot on and the farmer, had given us the `heads up` (notification) that a certain film star and very well-known personality was going to be over there just after first light with a few of his friends.

I actually knew the guy the farmer was talking about

and had done so for quite some time, so when Alan called to tell me about it and sounding excited, I said about going over there and surprising him.

It was only springtime, but the day dawned fine and by midday, it was an absolute scorcher. We were standing at the farm gate when Vinnie Jones and three of his pals turned up and the first words out of his smiling mouth to me was,

"What the f**k are you doing here?"

I explained that we, Alan and myself, had been shooting rabbits on this land for a few years now and then introduced Alan to him. I then explained that the farmer had told Alan of his coming and in turn, Alan had told me, and then I asked if it would be okay to hang about to see how ferreting should be done?

Now, the papers have in the past given Vinnie some bad press and in doing so he had acquired a tag in front of his name of; `Hard Man Vinnie Jones`.

Having known this guy personally for a while, as does my whole family, I can tell you that he is a really nice guy when out of the public eye and we all went on to have one of the best days ever.

Vinnie showed Alan and me just how to set the purse nets, how not to stamp all over the warren so as to frighten the rabbits therein and then, as we had our shotguns with us, we then acted as shooters for any rabbit that escaped the purse nets and tried bolting across the field when the ferrets were put down the hole.

Thinking that he might just stay a couple of hours, we ended up spending the whole day together. We shared our lunch with him and his mates and had a whole bunch of rabbits in the bargain.

He also had his young son's air rifle in his car and

happened to mention to me that he had been having real trouble zeroing the scope, so towards the end of the day, having been sunburned and really having enjoyed the whole affair, I said I would zero it for him, which I did. We had photos taken together and I asked him if it would okay to write an article on the day, to which he agreed and that was printed in The Shooting Times Magazine sometime after. Alan's photo of him and Vinnie sits proudly in Alan's living room as does the one of Alan and his first deer.

20

DARK WATERS

I had heard from someone or somewhere that there were some really nice carp in a small private lake and like the fish themselves, I took the bait!

Having found out where this place was and with some small degree of planning, I asked my wife, May to drop me off at 6 pm on the chosen night, and then to pick me up at the same time the following evening.

It was autumn and so the darkness of night came on early and I had about an hour or so to get my bearings, set up, and maybe start fishing before it became totally dark. Carrying the minimum amount of equipment, I climbed out of the car to cries from my young daughter at the time of .

"Don't go, Daddy! Don't leave my Daddy there Mummy!" and then I was gone.

The small lake was on the grounds of a private school and backed onto, of all things, a hospice. Trees and shrubs surrounded the lake but were not so thick as I could not move easily through and between them until I found a suitable spot to set up.

I had my trusty two-man ex-army bivvy (tent) with me, which took just a matter of minutes to erect being that it was no more than a sheet of canvas, two multi-piece poles and half a dozen thin metal pegs. There were two thin cord lines coming from the top of each pole, front and rear, and this prevented the whole thing from collapsing in on itself, but other than that, there was no groundsheet, and the thing was as basic as one could get.

I had owned it for years, and still favour the fact that it could have been `me` that started the trend of seeing so many small tents on beaches nowadays during the summer, as it used to be invaluable for eating lunch in and not getting sand blown into one's sandwiches or tea, and also proved really handy for changing into swimwear and drying off after a swim when others on the beach either tried to hide their embarrassment behind a useless windbreak or, as my folks did when taking my brother and me to the beach for the day; try and undress and dress with just a towel wrapped around us.

I set up the tent without clanking together the metal pegs, set up my rod and within just a short time was fishing.

It looked like good tench waters, with lots of greenery in the water and my immediate thought was that if I did get into a large carp, would I lose it in amongst all this weed and water lilies?

I had not been fishing long when suddenly I was in! The rod bowed, the line went taught and I landed, pulling it through this mass and tangle, a nice size tench.

Getting my keep net out, I placed the fish into it and it was now almost too dark to see without the use of a torch which I did not want to use for fear of being caught, so I decided I would climb into my bivvy, get an early night and start fishing again next morning as soon as it was light.

The night was not at all cold and the weather had been dry, so having no sleeping bag I just lay on the ground with my coat not on me, but over me, for I have noticed that this somehow keeps one warmer than if one was to just wear it.

With nothing to do, no book to read, TV to watch or radio to listen to, and it being so quiet in that little wood; it was not long before I was sound asleep.

I awoke and saw grey light at my feet and knew it was just after dawn. I had slept really well.

Climbing out of the tent, the first thing I noticed was the keep net. It looked as though someone had pulled it up by the wire rings that encircled it and kept it open, so that now, only the bottom two sections were still in the water and the fish I had caught the previous evening was now gone!

I was baffled by this as the fish could not have done it and I am sure that no one would have been around during the night without waking me and either kicking me off the property or arresting me. I puzzled this strange happening as I took down the tent and laid it out in readiness to fold it up. That's when I noticed the second thing. Earwigs! Lots of them!

I hate earwigs and with a love of cracks and crevices they had come into the tent whilst I had slept and were in the seam that ran the full six feet of its length. I suddenly felt as though I was crawling and started to take my top clothes off and shake them out and dropping my trousers, examining them too for any sign of the rotten little creepy crawlies. With a sigh of relief at not finding any on my person, it was far from a pleasant feeling to know that I had slept with these things all around me. Years later, I found one coming back in from shooting, which had got into, or under, one of my boot laces and that too freaked me out.

Having put the tent away, had a tea from my flask and a sandwich, I set about fishing for the day, trying still to fathom out the mystery of the keep net and the thought of earwigs. I had not been fishing for an hour, when standing there at the water's edge and quite still, I happened to look down and there, not three feet from me was sitting, on its haunches, like a cat; the biggest rat I have ever seen! It looked up at me, as if to say,

"Come on, I am waiting for you to catch my breakfast."

As I moved, likewise it did and was gone in a flash but then I saw another on the opposite bank. I have never, even to this day, seen rats that big before and I got to thinking whether it was one or more of these that had taken my fish from the keep net during the night?

I caught nothing, not a thing that day and quite honest could not wait until May came back and collected me. I have never been back to that lake, and I don't think that I will ever bother to either.

21

THE SPOOKY MANSION

All in all, I have had an interesting life and sometimes a very exciting life. Not just in my younger days with Roy, the jungle the marshes and the reservoirs nor even during my time in the army, where making sure I was the best I could possibly be, for survival reasons, I was nicknamed `Supersoldier` and having been on active service saw some action, and on more than a few occasions was lucky to have come home alive.

Without going into the nitty-gritty of it all, I one day found myself at Batsford House in the beautiful Cotswolds, and part of a training team, all ex-special and elite forces, putting a bunch of young wannabes through their paces in training them up to be spies for a TV reality programme called Spymaster.

As an instructor, during dinner one evening, I found myself sitting next to a guy that had been flown in from France to teach a particular type of martial art to the students called Krav Maga, which is based on an Israeli form of street fighting. He turned to me, passed me his business card and said, cheesily.

"We are always looking for a good man like you, if you feel the need, call me sometime."

This guy ran a security company based in Monte Carlo and sometime after the Batsford job, I did contact him and so began a life of security, bodyguarding stars, celebrities and the very rich.

The first job was a `freebie`, as this paid for the training that led up to it, and taking a group of seven guys over there, we had a fabulous time mixing with top stars from all around the world at the 2003 World Music Awards; and although the hours were very long and the training hard, we all did Krav Maga, pistol shooting and rifle firing during that time. I later, on returning to England obtained my SIA License as a Close Protection Front Line Operative (bodyguard) which is now required if working this side of the Channel.

Slightly prior to this though, I had a call from the security guy in France and flying out the very next day, found myself looking after a businessman that had been threatened at his chateau in Grasse, outside of Nice.

I was `tooled up` (armed) for the job, being that it was in France and although the principal had not been harmed, the job went horribly wrong, for reasons I am not saying and he and his family had to rapidly return to England and their mansion in the Berkshire countryside.

With my job and time having ended abroad, I too returned to England a few weeks later and then received another call from my French contact, saying that the mansion that my old principal now lived in, was in some kind of trouble, and could I get down there ASAP with a team of guys and secure it?

I went into action, not being able to get the full facts, and within a matter of just a few hours, had a team set up and ready to go, packed and loaded up for being able to block off and stay in the open for as long as need be to make the mansion and its grounds safe and secure.

Like many security jobs, or so I have since discovered, there tends to be a sudden rush, but not real panic, and then things cool off quite fast. This was much the same and rather than a whole bunch of us driving off into the night to we-knew-not-what, it rapidly calmed down and a much smaller team went along and began a security operation that was to last some time.

After a time, I managed to get Alan on this job and with the principal away most of the time, although having first gained his permission, we both ended up being able to shoot on this estate.

It was running alive with rabbit and pheasant and also some deer, when one day I spied a Reeves muntjac and during the daytime, I spent more time walking around the grounds with my rifle, than sitting inside where I had a flat inside the mansion with all mod cons.

The estate used to be massive in years gone by but much of it had now been sold off, but it still covered a good-sized area and when out with Alan, we had radio communication between us so as to report anything in the nature of the work we were doing, as well as any game we might have seen.

Alan radioed me from a slightly wooded area one evening just before dark.

"Alpha Foxtrot to Charlie Echo,"

"Charlie Echo, send."

"Alpha Foxtrot, have just shot the strangest looking deer? Not seen anything like it before!"

"Charlie Echo, wait one, am coming to your location."

"Alpha Foxtrot, roger that. Out"

When I found Alan, I could not see the thing he had been talking about on the radio at first, as it was lying dead in the undergrowth but when I did, and although I had not seen one before, or since, I knew straight away what it was. It was a Chinese water deer which he had dropped stone dead with a one-shot clean kill from his .22 rimfire.

Compared to the Reeves muntjac, it was a pretty thing, with a much longer looking neck and a prettier face. It reminded me slightly of a very small lama but the weirdest thing about it was its fur. It was like the fur one sees on a toy teddy bear and nothing like the fur or hair of any other deer.

Having had permission to shoot the rabbits and not the deer on the estate and not wishing the gardener to find it the next day, I told Alan he should dispose of it, put in his car boot and take it home.

Being a non-resident species, like the muntjac, the Chinese water deer is now also classed as a pest and therefore can be shot all year round in this country, but not, I hasten to add with a .22 rimfire rifle, even though it did the job cleanly and quickly.

The mansion was spooky, especially at night and even during daylight hours, it was cold inside, even in the middle of summer. The wind coming through an open window or door that had been left ajar played havoc with one's nerves and the alarm systems, and the guy that eventually took over from me; called me several times in his first few weeks of being there asking me how to shut off the alarms and whether he should venture out into the darkened corridors to see what had made a certain noise.

It had about eighty rooms, many of which were uninhabitable and once the alarms were set it was pointless going walk-about as one was alone there at night, so if one re-set them and they failed to set or were triggered again, it was best to just call the police and let them deal with whatever might be lurking in the dark shadows and recesses of that place.

There were great hopes on the owner's part of turning it into a five-star hotel but whether this ever came about I do not know? If it did, it would have cost an absolute fortune and that was long before the recession. It holds very fond memories for me though and it had some very fat rabbits living there.

PREPARATION AND COOKING

The following chapters of this book serve as my own humble ideas on how to prep and cook some of this quality, wild meat that I have spent most of my life hunting. I hope you find the recipes appealing, but do feel free to put your own twist on them!

RABBIT

Skinning a rabbit is about the easiest of animals to do as the skin comes off about as easy as a coat and with little resistance. This can be done in a variety of ways and the saying: ` There are many ways to skin a cat ` ; could equally apply to a rabbit.

I used to, having paunched (gutted) the rabbit in the field, tie it by its back legs and hang it from a hook or nail in a wall and then, cutting the skin around the rear ankles, peel the skin down until being able to get a good grip of fur and then simply pull down, over the rump, the body and ending at the neck and head. One can then remove the head and skin all in one go.

Another way and one I now find easier and if you have no need of the fur, is to lay the rabbit on the cutting board, face down, make a light cut across the back of the creature just through the skin and then, getting a grip of the two halves of coat, pull both halves away from each other, left and right with either hand so that the skin ends up at the head end in one hand and the feet end in the other. The head and feet can then be removed to leave just the flesh.

PORTIONING

Another thing I have changed over the years is the portioning of the meat. I used to take off the back legs at the joint and the front legs at the shoulder, all easily seen and then just cut through the body in two places, thereby giving me three equal pieces ready to be cooked. However, this also gave me many very small bones in the finished dish, and it could be this fact that puts many people off eating rabbits.

I now, still separate the rear and front legs as mentioned, but as far as the body meat is concerned, I cut down either side of the spine and so now get two very nice fillets about 6" long and an inch thick which can be used in a variety of ways and without any of the bones.

Apparently, during the war (WW11) and after, when food was rationed, a rabbit was a fine addition to the households' meat requirements and in town as well as in the country, someone looking to earn an extra shilling might come around selling these excellent beasts and offer them to the housewife.

I heard through my Nan that if anyone offered a

rabbit and the skin, head and feet had already been removed, the woman at the door would look inside the carcase at the animal's kidneys, for it is said that a rabbit's kidneys are offset and diagonal to each other, which they are, whereas a cat's kidneys are sited opposite each other inside the cavity. I am guessing by this fact, that cat and rabbit must not only look the same they must also taste very much the same.

RABBIT STEW
(BASIC)

Take one large rabbit portioned into 2 x back legs 2 x front legs and 2 x fillets cut into pieces.

One large onion.

One or two carrots cut into chunks.

One large potato cut into chunks.

A pint and a half of chicken or vegetable stock.

A few rashers of streaky bacon (if desired) cut into pieces.

Half a cup of pulses such as pearl barley, yellow split peas, marrowfat peas etc.

Seasoned flour.

Cooking oil. A splash.

Note: Other ingredients such as a tin of chopped tomatoes, red wine etc can be added to make the stew richer and fuller as well as some fresh herbs such as Thyme and Sage etc.

METHOD

Heat the oil in a pan, roll the rabbit in the seasoned flour, shake off excess and fry until sealed and golden brown. Remove from the pan and in the same oil, sweat off the onion until soft then add the bacon, the sealed rabbit the vegetables and the stock to cover.

Bring it to a boil and then add the pulses and keep the dish simmering hard for at least half-hour before turning it down to a lower heat. Stir frequently to prevent pulses from sticking to the base of the pot. Cooking time can be to suit. An hour to an hour and a half will suffice and any stew will always taste better if left to rapidly cool uncovered and then be reheated the following day.

Rabbit is a light meat, much like chicken, so any chicken recipe will do when cooking rabbit.

If one has a few rabbits, then one can portion them as mentioned and keep the leg joints for stews and casseroles and the fillets can be used the same as chicken breast meat and stir-fried, curried, or even cubed and placed on a skewer and cooked like a kebab. Fillet meat needs only minimal cooking as overcooking will make it tough.

VENISON

The meat of wild deer is rich, tasty and like most of God's creatures that run wild, virtually fat-free so many recipes will say add bacon or lardons. This, I think is a personal thing as adding bacon can take away the taste of the venison and like so much with cooking personal taste is what it is all about.

Skinning a deer is nothing like skinning a rabbit the knife has to be sharp and worked all the time and the skin is drawn away with the hand. Unless lucky enough to have been given a prepared piece of meat, the deer should be hung by its back legs from something that is secure enough to hold its weight and at a comfortable height.

With the chest or underside facing you and using a sturdy hunting knife, cut into the soft part of the belly just below the rib cage, trying not to puncture the guts if not already gralloched (gutted) in the field. Cutting through the ribs of say, a muntjac is not that difficult as they are cartilage rather than bone and very thin.

Once the chest is open, the weight of the innards will almost cause them to fall out and will only need lifting and cutting in the obvious places to remove them in one mass. Examine the liver and check for any signs of illness such as streaking or discolouring or spotting. If it looks as liver is supposed to look, then remove this along with the heart and kidneys and place it somewhere clean and cool.

Start skinning the animal by cutting from the ankle along the inside of the back legs towards the groin area and then peeling away and back, working your way around to the rear of the deer. Again, the weight of the skin coming away from the meat will assist you.

One can buy a Tee bar-shaped tool (plastic) that is used for removing the anus, failing this, it is not hard to cut out the anus or even leave it intact but making sure that any impurities do not come into contact with the meat of the two rear joints.

With the frequent sharpening of the knife, keep working at skinning the hide, around and down towards the neck and the back of the head, and then remove the head and skin as one. Should you wish to keep the skin for some purpose, be careful when skinning around the lower back area as the lack of flesh here makes it easy to cut holes in the hide, especially on a muntjac.

With the whole skin removed one can now portion up the carcase in readiness for cooking and storing.

Remove the hooves by either cutting through the joints or twisting them off or by sawing through them. Then cut around the shoulders of the front legs, easily seen by looking for where the shoulder blade is attached to the side of the chest. The two back fillets can then be removed the same as the rabbit, by working the knife down each side of the spine from rump to neck. Then the two roasting joints (back legs) can be cut away trying to keep as close as possible to the groin and hip. There are two inner fillets inside the carcase and attached to the spine, these are exceptionally good to eat but tend to be small and thin on a very small deer-like the Reeves muntjac.

Removing the head and attached hide, gives you easy access to the neck which can be cut away from the remains of the body then portioned ready for making your venison stew. Any remaining meat, such as the thin belly meat I cook up for the dog, but this too could be added to a stew or casserole.

Hanging the carcass or even freezing the prepared meat it will tenderise it. If hanging, this should be done before skinning it and should be in a fly-free environment or covered with say a piece of net curtain or mosquito netting to prevent flies from getting to it and left this way for a week or two.

The bright red meat one sees in a supermarket may look right and appetising but taste-wise, darker looking meat comes out tops every time.

Roasting a muntjac joint should only take about 45 minutes, middle shelf at 200F and can be placed on a bed of cut onions, carrots, parsnips and topped with a couple of sprigs of thyme for that special dinner. Red wine, juniper berries and caramelised onions will all add to and enhance the flavour and richness of the dish.

PIGEON

Woodpigeon is very dark meat. Looking much like liver when uncooked but tastes like best steak once cooked off.

One gets about 4 ounces of fat-free dark meat from a single bird and because it is rich meat, just a brace of pigeons will make a fulfilling meal for any man. A pigeon was the first wild meat I ever tasted and over the years, like a rabbit, I have now eaten this in every way possible.

Just flash-frying it is fabulous for a Sunday morning breakfast and I tend to having removed the breasts from the carcase, cut them in half through their thickness, butterflying them so making two breast halves into four but only half as thick. This way they cook quicker, and it looks as though there is more on the plate.

Just a couple of minutes frying on each side in a hot pan with a dash of oil and butter is all that's needed and to make it into a proper Sunday fry up, one can add a handful of chopped mushrooms too and with a couple of free-range eggs; what could be better?

If one removes the crown, leaving both breasts

attached to the ribs, it is easy to store in the freezer and ideal for dishes such as casseroles and stews. With all that goes into such a one-pot dish, just one crown per person along with the vegetables, pulses and gravy and maybe a few boiled potatoes, make a heart-warming dish on a cold winter's night and a splash of red wine in the dish, stew or casserole, makes it even richer and rather special.

GAME PIE

By cutting the meat from deer, pigeon, pheasant and rabbit into small pieces and pan-fry them for a minute or two with chopped onion and then add chopped vegetables and rich gravy and allow the mixture to cool. One has the makings of a game pie. Again, add some good red wine, a small sprig of thyme, spoon into a suitable oven-proof dish and cover with either shortcrust or puff pastry and bake for 30 minutes, middle shelf at 200 F or until pastry browns. Diced potato mixed with the other vegetables in the dish will thicken the gravy and a knob of butter will enrich it.

All these dishes are relatively quick and easy to prepare and cook and if one bought them in a restaurant, one would pay considerable high prices for them. I was once charged almost £ 5.00 just for a starter of pigeon and all I got dished up was one half of one breast, just 2 ounces!

I was sorely tempted to ask," What happened to the other half?" and would have done but for embarrassing my fellow diners.

I think it is the butchery side of things that puts many off eating game, but once over this problem or phobia, the meal is a pleasant change from the shop-bought meats of chicken, lamb, beef, and pork and so adds variety. As already mentioned, wild meat from these animals is fat-free, so therefore very healthy and none of them has been pumped full of `E` numbers, preservatives, water or anything that is not natural. The texture is different from shop-bought meat too. Rabbit for instance, for those that have never eaten it; is much like chicken but much firmer. Pigeon is far denser than say steak, and both pheasant and partridge are light meats needing little cooking time to make them taste delicious.

WITH THE END IN SIGHT

And so, I have covered my youth and days of poaching on Walthamstow Marshes and Reservoirs, of shooting pheasants in the fields of Essex and of being chased by the police and of having been caught, and being let off for reasons not known?

I have matured much over the last forty years and now shoot responsibly, legally and with insurance. I have been so lucky to have enjoyed such adventures and tried to share some of them with you and I still have adventures to this day, as ` life is what you make it.

THE SALT BEEF SANDWICH
A CHERISHED MEMORY

I mentioned in this book that after a couple of hours of pigeon shooting on a Sunday morning over the Walthamstow Marshes and reservoirs, we, the band of men that carried out such deeds then retired to Nan` s Cafe`, later known as The Woodman, to enjoy a Sunday morning breakfast of bacon butties or a good fry up with dogs, wet and muddy boots and guns openly strewn all over the place.

However, there were other times when just Roy and me used to wander back into Stamford Hill through Clapton and there found a small shop that did the most delicious salt-beef sandwiches.

Stamford Hill and some of the surrounding area is home to a large Jewish community and because of their religious convictions, they are forbidden to eat ham or any pork-based produce. This is where salt beef comes into being as it is beef so prepared that it tastes much like best ham and is usually served warm and plentiful in thick bread. If one has never tasted a salt-beef sandwich, then you really have missed out on one of life's delicacies.

I remember not only the deliciously warm and fulfilling sandwiches on those cold winter mornings there with my best friend in that little delicatessen, but also the feeling of togetherness and the sharing that came with it.

We used to laugh and tell tales of the shoot, the banter that came with the end of any shoot. We used to reminisce and laugh over what one or more of the other men had said or done, not only on that day but at other times and many of the stories were told repeatedly.

They were very special times and moments for me and I guess for Roy also because very many years later, shortly before Christmas 2015 when, now stricken with prostate cancer in his home in Cambridge; his wife called me late one evening and said that he had asked her to call me and say that he wanted me to get him a salt-beef sandwich, and would I ask for it to be triple wrapped so that it would still be warm when I delivered it to him.

I still live in London and not that far from Walthamstow and the reservoirs where we walked and fished and shot which makes it a good one and half hours' drive from my house to his, and being that the call had been so late in the evening, I immediately asked whether he was alright and if it was a wind-up or if he was joking?

"Oh! don't take it too seriously," she said, her voice and tone sounding light and unperturbed, "you know what he's like." The following day was December 23rd, the day before Christmas Eve, and I had thought late into the previous night about that call and the request for the sandwich.

The following morning, I found a delicatessen not too far away from where I live and bought freshly cooked, salt-beef sandwiches, had them triple wrapped and then set off directly to his address up the M11 and A14 to where he lived with his wife in a beautiful cottage at the end of a remote drove where the road ends and the fields begin.

It was late morning when I arrived and was greeted by his wife who, as always never seemed swayed and when I said that I had bought along the sandwiches he had asked for the previous evening, she smiled, chuckled lightly and told me that she was sure he would enjoy like them and like to see me.

He had been confined to his sickbed for quite some time, now hardly leaving it to venture outside and to walk his beloved lake that he had so painstakingly had made and stocked with carp. I had on previous visits told him he should try and get out a little more just to feel the grass beneath his bare feet and to this, he smiled and had said nothing.

I entered the bedroom, presented him with the food, still warm and he smiled once more hardly being able to open his eyes.

"Hey," he said, his voice weak trying to raise himself up on his many pillows. I could hardly speak.

"Hey, I replied, "how are you mate?"

He just smiled again as I handed him the sandwiches.

His wife entered the room and I said that I would be in the kitchen. I stood there for what seemed ages just staring out of the window, silently crying and thinking.

At long last, she returned and spoke to me in that unmoving steady voice of hers that hid so well what she was truly feeling.

"He enjoyed those sandwiches." she said, "he ate almost all of them."

I had not related the meaning of them, the times just the two of us had enjoyed them together so very many years before, and that he must have been thinking of me, of us, when he had asked her to call me the night before and to get them for him.

"That's good. "I said, forcing a smile.

I then returned to where he lay, took his hand, and now with eyes closed again he smiled.

"Love you man." I said, my voice sounding croaky.

"Love you too." he said softly and squeezed my hand, but his grip had no strength in it. I could not say anymore. I had to go. I let slip his grip, kissed him on the forehead wanting to embrace him, hold him tight, but I didn't, I just left the room told his wife I had to go and then left, knowing that I would never see him again.

I cried all the way back to London as rain lashed against the windscreen and the spray from the motorway traffic made it even harder for me to see. I had already lost a very dear and long-time friend at the beginning of December and now it looked as though I would soon lose another, my very best and dearest friend, Roy.

He made it through Christmas, we both did, but then on January 3rd 2015, just a week before his birthday and two weeks before mine, he died where I had last seen him, in that bed in the cottage.

I had loved him most of my life, as he was like the older brother I had never had and although even now, a year on, I still miss him greatly and always will, I hated seeing him suffer the way he must have done towards the end, but that simple request for that silly salt-beef sandwich holds so many dear and loving memories for me.

DEDICATION AND THANKS

I would like to dedicate this book firstly to Roy Whitehall, my very dear friend and mentor and a man who showed me the ways of fieldcraft and introduced me to the great outdoors. Who taught me how to shoot and fish and be at one with nature.

I would like all the shooting men of Walthamstow Marshes and Reservoirs to be remembered, whether alive or dead, and please forgive me if I have missed out any names:

Steve Hume
Albie Challis
Jimmy Bradshaw
Charlie Brownlow
Chrissy Bland
Ginger/Archie
Yogi
Black Powder Pete
Bill Reilly
Clifford Lawrence
Alan Konway
Alan and Jeff Simons

...And the Water-board men, who we must have tested, but also respected.

I make a special mention here to, Keith Sullivan and

Alan Frith long-time friends and shooters and who, like me, have seen the sun and moon rise and set on still waters and over wintry marshes heard the songbirds sing their chorus when all others have still been sleeping.

I would like to give thanks for all the support I received in writing this account from family and friends, and especially my son, Cheynne who dedicated his time in designing the cover for this book.

FINALLY...

I lost touch with Roy for very many years for reasons I am not prepared to mention here, but having found him again in more recent years, we were still the best of friends, better in fact, until his sad death on January 3rd, 2015, when he sadly lost his long fight to prostate cancer.

I mentioned earlier that I would say more about Lenny Middleton. When he died of a heart attack in 2006, he left a legacy. All his finely detailed fishing records as well as, very many photos to Roy, and he in turn, had them passed onto me via his widow.

Besides being just a very nice guy, Lenny was also a first-class fisherman, as well as the falconer I knew him to be, and for those of you that are `keen carp anglers,` he was also the inventor of the `Hair Rig`, now famous world-wide to every carp fisherman.

If I should ever find the time to plough through the oh so much information, I may attempt to write it up somehow and get it out there to those of you that might be interested in reading such matter.

ROY

Born: Roy Richard Whitehall, January 9th, 1943
Died: John Phillips, January 3rd, 2015

Roy Whitehall became a world-renowned taxidermist although for reasons unknown to many, changed his name more than once.

He was I would say, first a born naturalist then a more than keen fisherman, and finally a cracking shot with both shotgun and rifle. He hunted all over the world, stuffed and mounted everything from fish and small mammals to big cats, wildebeests and bears and lived the life that he chose.

To some, if not most, he was something of an `enigma` and would have been a hundred different people to a hundred different people.

I was proud to be there at the beginning of his taxidermy career and at his end, and for that, I will always be grateful, as to me he was like a brother, and I loved him like one as he did me.

ROY

An Ode

Save me a place by the water's edge, dear friend, where once again we may fish.
Save me a place in the sun, dear friend, where once again we may stand with a gun,
And I will save a place for you in my heart, dear friend until my days are done!